MARYJANE'S
OUTPOST

UNLEASHING
YOUR
INNER

wild

MARYJANE'S OUTPOST

UNLEASHING YOUR INNER *wild*

MaryJane Butters

CLARKSON POTTER/PUBLISHERS
NEW YORK

Published in the United States by Clarkson Potter/Publishers, an imprint of the Crown Publishing Group, a division of Random House, Inc., New York.
www.crownpublishing.com
www.clarksonpotter.com

Clarkson N. Potter is a trademark and Potter and colophon are registered trademarks of Random House, Inc.

With the exception of the photographs by MaryJane Butters, all photographs are credited as follows:

Photo on p. 6 (bottom), copyright © Tasha-Rose Mirick. Photos on p. 7 (far right), p. 125, p. 126, p. 127 (left), and p. 129 copyright © Doug Keister. Photos on p. 10, p. 50, p. 226, and p. 240 (right), copyright © Patrick Bennett. Photo on p. 51, copyright © Michael Gallacher/Missoulian. Photos on p. 123 (right), and p. 124 (top left), copyright © USC Special Collections. Photo on p. 123 (far right), copyright © Tumbleweed Tiny House Company. Photo on p. 146, copyright © Corinna Raznikov. Photo on p. 164, copyright © Dave Schiefelbein. Photo on p. 166, copyright © www. istockphoto.com.

Cataloging-in-Publication Data is available from the Library of Congress.

ISBN: 978-0-307-34580-6

Printed in the United States of America

Art Direction by MaryJane Butters and Carol Hill
Design by Carol Hill

All of us at MaryJanesFarm welcome your comments and suggestions. Write to us at iris@maryjanesfarm.org or visit us on the Web at www.maryjanesfarm.org and www.maryjanesoutpost.org.

1 2 3 4 5 6 7 8 9 10

First Edition

A U T H O R ' S   N O T E

Like "puttin' up hay" to satisfy a hunger, I couldn't wait to get this book "baled up" and into your hungry hands. Now I'm stompin' like a keyed-up pony, eager to hear the story of how you caught your first fish, landed your outdoor dream job, purchased a vintage teardrop trailer, walked thirty miles with a toddler on your back, fixed up an old truck "bed" for a romantic getaway, or camped alone. Tell me the reaction you got at the office when you showed up with a hatbox-turned-picnic-basket full of cheap bling, vintage metalware, wild edibles, and homemade dandelion wine to celebrate a co-worker's birthday. Tell me what it felt like when you took your first "heart shot" and a four-point buck dropped. And when I'm old and gray, tell me this book turned your daughter into an author because you started reading to her every day under a "story tree." Tell me your granddaughter wants to work for the Forest Service, "just like MaryJane did." Tell me I'm the reason you pulled your bedding out the back door last night. Tell me I've helped you set new boundaries beyond and outside what you once thought were possible. Tell me. Share your stories on my Outpost Dispatch, www.maryjanesoutpost.org … the place where "out there" women post online.

CONTENTS

INTRODUCTION
Outthinking

> 66 *It is written*
> on the arched sky;
> it looks out from every star.
> It is the poetry of Nature;
> it is that which uplifts
> the spirit within us. 99
>
> – John Ruskin

This book is dedicated to
my mother, Helen,
who made a rare, out-of-the-ordinary vow
to "grow-me-up" outdoors; to
my daughter, Meg,
who gave me the opportunity to pass
the favor and fervor along; and to
my granddaughter, StellaJane,
for giving me the opportunity to see the
"raising Jane" story repeat itself.

Aunt Lois and Helen, 1960

MaryJane and Meg, 2005

What are you waiting for?

Surely, the romance of the outdoors is better than the latest movie, an iPod whatever, a video game victory, or the "thrill" of yet another restaurant meal.

Why sit around indoors when you can invite your friends, young and old, to a unique picnic? Not only do people bond better without a roof over their heads, you don't have to vacuum the floor afterwards. Why sleep inside, bound by walls, when your backyard or rooftop has a ceiling of twinkling lights, a "room" where once a month the moon is so bright you'd swear it was a reading light?

Having lived outdoors as a Utah wilderness ranger, Idaho fire lookout, Snake River ranch hand, Salmon River milkmaid, Teton Mountain fence builder, and more, I'll show you exactly how, now. You won't need to wait until you can buy expensive, fancy equipment. And I won't leave you on your own either. I'll help you get ready for "more outdoor" as we get better acquainted and you get more comfortable. We'll take it one step at a time, with plenty of tips on how to get your kids out the door too.

First, in OUTTHINKING, you'll merely think and get inspired about what's out there.

In OUTBOUND, you'll head to your porch, yard, or rooftop using some innovative ideas you never knew existed. After that, you'll get more confident—even kicking up a little sass along the way.

In OUTRIGGED, you'll join the ranks of "reel women" who go tramping (trailer camping), and glamping (glamour camping). You'll motor somewhere out-of-town in outrageous style "sporting" accessories you've made yourself, like an "alluring" pair of earrings made from fishing lures. Or you'll go "trolling" using a lantern chandelier made from fishing tackle (with outdoor safety advice on how to avoid "lunkers" of the two-legged variety).

In OUTSTEPPING, you'll turn hard core, grab a backpack, and head out for a seven-day trip "Alone at Last," relying on my unique high-protein meal plan that won't break the bank or your back.

And sprinkled throughout are the inspirational stories of OUTSPOKEN women who've blazed the trail and beyond. Read and be inspired.

By the time you turn the last page, your inner wild will be OUT, footloose and fancy-free. I flat-out guarantee it!

OUTTHINKING

Haven't we all heard by now how important it is to eat a diet high in roughage? Likewise, "roughaging" (spending time outdoors) is essential to our *mental* health. Even if it's a settee on the porch, we need it. Gotta have it ...

PLANTING SEEDS

I'm going to ask you to be a pretend farmer for a couple of minutes and sprout a little thought. It's the kind of thought that will set you on your way to becoming a nature girl, a camper, an outside mama, an outpost maitre d', a hardcore mountain climber, a weekend tailgater, a paid naturalist, a backwoods ranger, a river guide, an outfitter ... whatever it is you want. If you're already comfortable being outside, you'll know the kind of thought I'm about to plant, a tiny seed that grows and grows.

Okay, here's a thought, an image, a fantasy. You're alone somewhere in the outback. You're driving a vintage (insert favorite make and color) pickup truck. For this fantasy, "she" runs like a spurred sorrel and never gives you any trouble. You're driving down a dirt road; it's summer, but not too hot, just right. The wind

"*What is life* but what a [wo]man is thinking all day?"
– Ralph Waldo Emerson

You pull up to a river and turn off your engine. You'll unhook and "level 'er up" later, pull out your awning, set up your chair. Right now the fish might be biting.

is blowing your hair. You reach up and adjust the wing window to take in even more air and the muscle in your arm flexes. You smile. Your well-earned laugh lines get in on the act too. You see a tiny town up ahead so you start shifting down, but first you check for that familiar glint of silver in your rearview mirror. She's pulling just fine. "Girlfriend" follows you everywhere, whenever you get that *urge*—the urge to go it alone. Or not. Sometimes you take your kids, grandkids, a partner. Sometimes you meet up with other tramps (trailer campers). Alone doesn't have to be your choice all the time, as long as you own up to the urge and the title to the trailer is in your name.

You pull up in front of the town's general store, grab your hat off the seat, and step out and into … your next fantasy.

"Got any night crawlers?" you ask the young gal who's already seriously wondering what you're about. Everything else you already have in tow behind you—the beauty of a trailer (or a pickup truck with a camper or shell). Your stuff is always packed and ready to go.

Now you've just planted another seed, this time in someone else—the young gal who checked you out and spied your rig out front. Here's what she saw:

Either a woman completely unafraid of being alone or doing her darndest to confront head-on her "alone-out-there" fears. She sensed your strength. She envied your spirit. Your gumption. She asked, "Where you from?" She wanted to know more. Like most of us, she favors independence over dependence. It's a contagious thing, independence. The minute you see it, you want it for yourself. As you leave with your fishing bait, another new seed is already sprouting.

You pull up to a river and turn off your engine. You'll unhook and "level 'er up" later, pull out your awning, set up your chair. Right now the fish might be biting. They've got a primal hunger too. Yours, though, is satisfied for now—until the next time, and the next outpost urge grabs you.

I wrote this book to nurture and grow the outdoor seed in you, to get you "out there." I hope it's just the nudge you needed. And if you're a well-seasoned outdoor gal like me (and we are *not* tough old broads—I'm as tender-hearted as they come), I've sprinkled in lots of new and useful outpost know-how for all types, from beginner to fully busted out.

LIVING WITH NATURE

When wild taps me on the shoulder,
I stop to listen, lean, and then linger long on the tall handle of a hoe. We are, after all, composed of the same elements as soil—our final home as well—so it is a homecoming when someone decides to farm or garden.

For a farmer, wild is a neighbor, leaning over the fence to say hello all day long. It's why I chose an agrarian life some twenty years ago. Wild has turned me into an empiricist, and sometimes, like this morning, a lyricist. I always have its companionship in the moon, the wind, a soft place to nap outside, a walk alone at night, and my own two feet. Granted, farming isn't easy, but the work has taught me that easy comes from hard. In a farmer's hand, a vegetable seed is small and hard. Planting a tiny heirloom tomato seed that will someday send my salivary glands into an ecstatic spasm is the perfect example of wonderful that comes from hard. And every season it starts again, in the dark, in the soil. A seed is just a tiny little bit of hope, with wild still inside it. Will it sprout and take hold?

When wild taps me on the shoulder, I stop to listen, lean, and then linger long on the tall handle of a hoe. We are, after all, composed of the same elements as soil—our final home as well—so it is a homecoming when someone decides to farm or garden. Only dirty, calloused hands and a tired back can help us remember what really matters. It's no wonder the corporate manager and the banker are so often homesick, threatening to cash in their chips and buy a farm.

If you believe in such things as a soul, a farm is good for it. I'm as goal-oriented as the next person, but in my setting at the end of a dirt road, wild stops me from letting the clock run my life. She's a great teacher.

Last week, early one morning, I decided to check up on our honeybees by putting an ear to each side of their hives. The louder the hum from inside, the healthier the hive, indicating there's a strong queen and many worker bees. Just beyond our hives lay a jumble of firewood, mauls, and axes—a work in progress, one of my son's projects. The morning sun was warm, so I found two bolts of unsplit firewood, one for a seat and one for a back cushion, and sat a spell, putting my face to the sun, closing my eyes.

It never fails. Once my eyes are closed, I begin to hear something other than the chatter in my head. In the distance, my husband was talking to Esme and Angie, our cows, as he fed and patted them. "Co' boss! co' boss!" As the heat warmed the pine logs surrounding me, I could smell their pitch, the intoxicating smell that household cleaners try in vain to mimic. I heard what I thought must be a mouse moving busily in the grass two feet away. I opened my eyes to confirm that my senses were still sharp. My chickens were scratching in the dirt around me, completely focused, as if their lives depended on it—which not so very long ago, as wild birds, they did. I dialed in on the twittering of songbirds. A nearby woodpecker sounded off like a coiled spring let loose. I was savoring the moment when a pack of coyotes hit the airwaves, wailing and yelping, one of the more bizarre sounds wild has to offer. It was out of the ordinary: Around here, coyotes never yelp during the day. As Esme bellowed back at them and a honeybee flew by, I thought, I've got it all.

OUTBOUND

Going Wild RIGHT OUTSIDE Your Door

"*Prowling* his own quiet backyard or asleep by the fire, he is still only a whisker away from the wilds."

– Jean Burden

IN THIS CHAPTER

19

The Weather's Warm
& THE BACKYARD CALLS ...

OUTPOST PORCHES

After I lost my turn-of-the-century farmhouse in a fire in 1996, I was desperate to set up house again, no matter how small. In make-do style, I converted an old shed into my temporary home. The most important feature I couldn't be without was a "sittin' porch," complete with summer kitchen.

If your house doesn't have a front porch, think of other ways to spend time out front. It may be as simple as extending your front steps and adding a wooden porch onto the front of the house. Perhaps a more natural "patio" under some nearby trees would suffice. Move your chairs and try it out. How about a sitting area surrounded by a nibbling garden, or maybe a couple of swinging loveseats with awnings? Invite your neighbors over with the promise of food, take your kitchen chairs outside, and start brainstorming. Whatever you decide, your daily life is more likely to include other people if you spend time outdoors rather than hidden away inside.

" *A perfect summer day* is when the sun is shining, the breeze is blowing, the birds are singing, and the lawn mower is broken. "

– James Dent

AFTER

21

Furniture stock ... right outside my door!

OUTPOST FURNISHINGS

When I set up temporary housekeeping in the old shed pictured on the previous page, the first thing I did was plant a lilac bush on each end of the porch and the fastest-growing willow tree I could find on the south side. Within two years, the willow tree was providing abundant shade. Twelve years later, the tree I planted (www.austree.com) not only gives me ample shade, it's also a source of wood for making willow furniture, everything from miniature pinkeepers and doll furniture to adult chaise lounges and tables and chairs. It also feeds the occasional moose.

When making willow furniture, it's best to work without any kind of blueprint, but to get you started, I've outlined some steps for building a simple end table. I've also included some photos of willow furniture for inspiration. Besides a milk crate with a pillow on top, willow or driftwood furniture is the easiest kind of outside furniture you can build, since it doesn't require any kind of power tools beyond a small drill.

A twig bed that doubles as a pinkeeper!

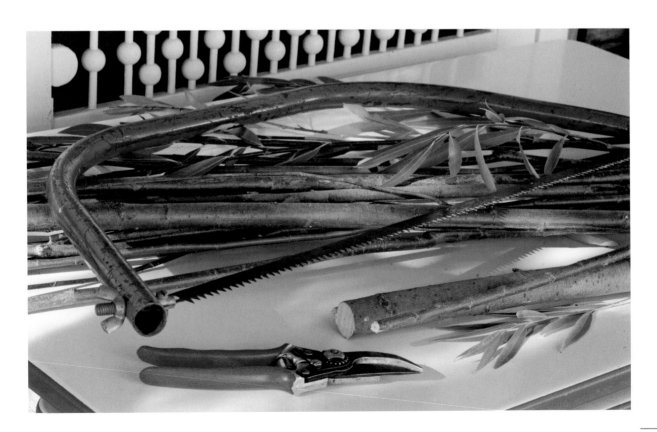

Make a Willow Table

Time: approximately 4 hours
Skill Level: beginner–intermediate (you just need to be able to use a hand saw, drill, and screwdriver)

Willow:

Gather willow branches, remove all limbs and cut to the specified lengths. (Note: All diameter measurements are rough averages, so just get as close as you can.) Sand all rough edges smooth. Separate your wood into like sizes. (Double-check your willow legs to make sure that all four are the same length.)

4	1 1/2" diameter x 26" willow branches
30	1/2" diameter x 16" willow branches
4	1/4" diameter x 18" green willow branches
4	1/4" diameter x 15" green willow branches
2	1/4" diameter x 36" green willow branches

Supplies and Tools:

Pruning shears
Hand or table saw
Measuring tape
Drill
Screwdriver or screwdriver bit for your drill
Level
Sandpaper
1" and 1 1/2" screws (longer screws are used for attaching braces to legs; all other pieces are assembled using 1" screws)
Fine 3/4" nails (for attaching the green willow)

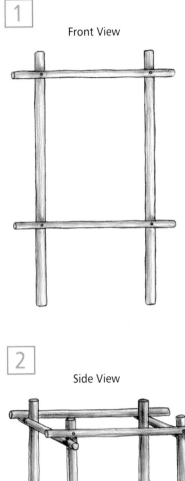

1

Front View

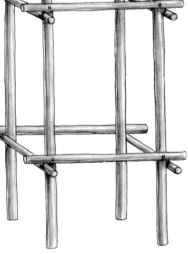

2

Side View

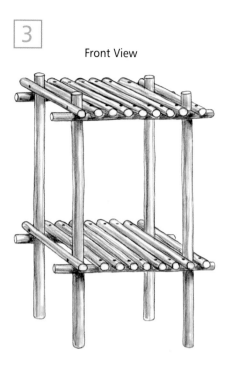

Front View

3

Instructions:

Note: Pre-drill all holes so the wood doesn't split.

1. Using two of the 1 1/2" x 26" pieces for the legs and two of the 1/2" x 16" pieces for the braces, attach the braces to the legs. For the top brace, drill the holes 2" down from the top and 2" in from each end. For the bottom brace, drill holes 8" up from the bottom and 2" in from each end. Repeat for second frame.

2. Join the two side panels with four additional cross braces, resting them atop the first pairs as shown.

3. Place seven 1/2" x 16" pieces parallel to the topmost braces, between the legs, to make a top shelf, spaced roughly 1" apart. Repeat to make a lower shelf.

4. Using eight of the 1/2" x 16" pieces, add a second layer of braces above each shelf, following placements in drawing.

5. Gently bend the 1/4" x 36" willow pieces to shape for the large arches and attach to the bottom shelf. Do the same with the 1/4" x 15" and 1/4" x 18" willow pieces for the layered arches on the top shelf and attach as shown.

4

Front View

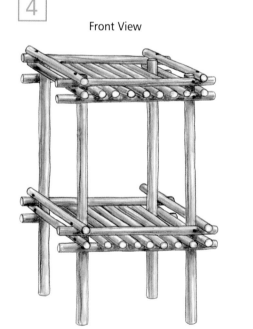

5

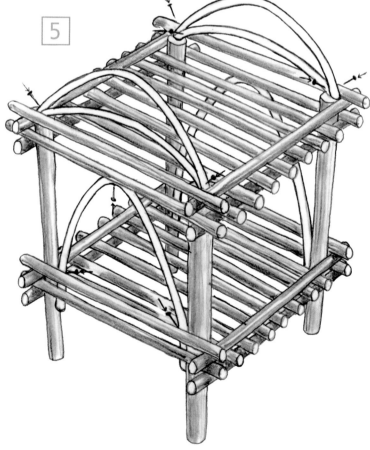

"*Wherever you go,* no matter what the weather, always bring your own sunshine. "

– Anthony J. D'Angelo

Personalize your outdoor world with a place to rest, a spot for books, or the romance of nature in a fence gone wild.

OUTPOST BEDS

Twenty years ago, when I was a single mom with two little kids, my lofty dreams for the future seemed permanently on hold as I coped with a series of low-paying jobs, broken cars, and skinned knees.

My urge to escape first grabbed me in the middle of the night and the dead of winter. I had the uncontrollable urge to escape outside. It just couldn't wait until morning. I grabbed a pillow and a down sleeping bag, and leaving my children sleeping safely in their beds, I went into my backyard.

I made myself a bed on one of those silly cheap plastic chaise lounges beneath my children's bedroom window and settled in, still within earshot. Once the magical warmth of down feathers kicked in and I quit shivering, I noticed my new ceiling: millions upon millions of stars, the whole universe, galaxies and beyond.

Almost immediately, the round-and-round chatter in my head started shifting gears. I remember how beautiful the moon looked. "Good grief," I laughed to myself, "my problems aren't more important than the moon!" I felt diminished in a way that gave me immediate relief from the small stuff that tends to loom larger than life when you lose perspective and manmade walls and concerns close in on you.

As our lives become more and more hectic, more "modern," it becomes harder to find time to spend outdoors in nature's clearinghouse. We must sleep, though, and sleeping outside, or at least next to an open window, helps us get a much-needed fix of nature every day. If you're the multitasker type, it's the perfect solution, accomplishing a dose of outdoors while sleeping. Outside is a lifeline. It just is. Our evolutionary molecules crave it. Children especially need it, but problem-solving adults can certainly benefit from it too. It's a simple solution to some of what ails us. Summers are meant for sleeping outdoors. Let nature fill you with its sweepstakes. You'll wake up a winner.

Keeping Bugs at Bay

There aren't many mosquitoes where I live, but it only takes one to rob me of a good night's sleep. Mosquito netting can be as simple and cheap as an old sheer curtain draped over your headboard, or it can be a full-size, store-bought canopy (www.mombasausa.net). Style-wise, a mosquito canopy will give your outdoor bed an elegant look. Since the air here is seldom still, my outdoor beds are like graceful dancers always in motion. They certainly add panache to my farm, inviting me to lie back and dream.

Build an Outpost Canopy

Time: approximately 8 hours
Skill Level: intermediate

Supplies and Tools:

11 2" x 2" x 8' framing lumber, grade No. 1
1   1" x 2" x 8' framing lumber, grade No. 1
3   2" x 2" x 10' framing lumber grade No. 1
1/2 lb 1 1/2" screws or nails
1   lb 3" screws
1/4 lb 1" brads
3/8" staples
24" plumber's tape or hanger iron
1   8' x 10' waterproof canvas, unhemmed
36' 1/4" x 1 1/2" wood lath or screen molding
50' galvanized wire or baling wire (optional)

Measuring tape
Hand or table saw
Hammer
Framing square
Heavy-duty staple gun
Razor
Level

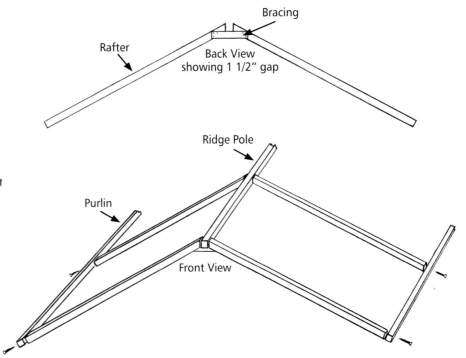

Rafter

Bracing

Back View
showing 1 1/2" gap

Ridge Pole

Purlin

Front View

Instructions:

1. Using the 2" x 2" x 8' lumber, cut 10 rafters, 44 1/2" in length, each with one 24° end.

2. Using the 1" x 2" x 8' lumber, cut 5 bracing pieces, 8" in length.

3. Nail or screw a bracing piece between two of the rafters at the 24° end, leaving a 1 1/2" gap for the ridge to fit into (the rafters should be 80" apart at the bottom). Make 5 of these.

4. Using the 2" x 2" x 10' lumber, cut one ridge pole and two purlins, each 117" in length. Position the rafter units on the ground as they would look on the finished canopy, spacing them 29 1/4" on center, and insert the ridge pole in the top gaps. Nail or screw purlins along the bottom of the rafter ends, so the rafters are again 29 1/4" on center.

5. Using the 2" x 2" x 8' lumber, cut two stringers 81" in length and notch with a framing square (90°) with a 24° offset. These keep the purlins from spreading apart. A strong union can be made using a 6" length of perforated metal plumber's tape wrapped around the purlin and screwed to the stringer a couple of times (as shown in the detail drawing of the stringer joining the purlin). This union should be just behind the first and last rafters.

6. Cover the rigid roof frame with canvas, keeping it square and taut. Staple securely at least every inch around the outer perimeter. This stapled perimeter can be then covered with the lath or molding using brads. Trim canvas neatly with a razor after fastening lath or molding.

7. Using the 2" x 2" x 8' lumber, cut 4 columns, 78" in length. The columns should be "pinned" to the stringers several inches in from the roof eaves, using 3" screws or nails. (The lengths of the columns may vary if the ground is not level.)

Note: 6" of each column will be set into the ground. The best way to do this is to bury a piece of 2" pipe into the ground, then insert the end of the column into it.

8. If your canopy is surrounded by trees, you can brace it further by running guy wires from the outside rafters or columns to the trees.

This rendition of an outpost canopy was sent to me by a woman in Montana who had visited my farm. Inspired by my canvas outpost canopies, she built herself a lodge-pole structure with a permanent floor and metal roof for her outpost bed.

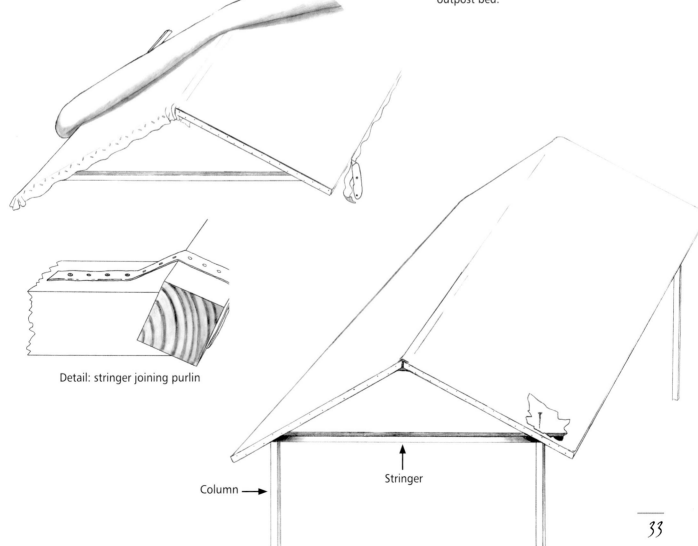

Detail: stringer joining purlin

Column →

↑
Stringer

"The basic aid to *feminine daintiness,* a good soaking bath, ofttimes was one of the rarest luxuries, achieved only by the most determined of the sex."

– Dee Brown, *Gentle Tamers—Women of the Wild West*

OUTPOST
BATHING

Can you imagine anything more luxurious, more indulgent, than bathing in the open air? Rarely in today's society do we get to be so carefree. There's something liberating about revealing our skin to Mother Nature. She is gracious and accepting; she makes us feel at home, just as we are. So why not create an idyllic outpost bath where you can soak up nature's graces?

First, determine if you have a spot suited to an outdoor tub. Even in populated areas, a simple fence, hedge, or privacy screen can offer sweet seclusion. If your surroundings are utterly urban, you can "untame" your private bathing area with lush potted plants—even trees.

The next consideration is the bathtub itself. Any home supply store can sell you an expensive hot tub, which will need to have its water continually purified, sometimes with toxic chemicals. Another unique outdoor tub option is the Dutchtub (www.dutchtub.com), a whimsical, lightweight, fire-fueled tub that was designed to "create an outdoor bathing culture." A much simpler solution is to search architectural salvage yards for a romantic vintage claw-foot tub.

Think of your cast-iron bathtub as a giant cast-iron cooking pot. You can simply build a wood fire under the tub to heat the water, but I built a permanent "fire" using a propane camp stove.

I fill the bathtub with fresh water from a garden hose, light the burners underneath the tub, then check the water temperature in about two hours (depending on the temperature outside). If you want to speed this process up, you can put some sort of insulated panel on top of your tub (I put a piece of plywood on top covered with a quilt). Once I'm ready for my bath, I turn off both burners and hop in (I touch the bottom of the tub to make sure it's not too hot and don't ever step directly on top of the burner areas). If the water is too hot, I use my hose to add a little cold water.

Solitude? What's that?
Not long ago, I realized how much of my life was filled with NOISE, the noise of the radio in the car on my commute to work, the sound of the overhead radio at work and the constant background noise of other coworkers talking, the click, click of the key on the computer keyboard all day ... and then at night as I surf the net, the sound of the dishwasher or washer going in the background, the overhead sound of the radio as you shop in any store ... noise, noise, noise, everywhere ... where does one get a moment of silence?? I long for some solitude and quiet in my life ... so I am trying to make changes, like I don't listen to a radio on my way to work, small changes that I hope will help clear the noise in my life. "

– Michelle
MaryJane's Farmgirl Connection
www.maryjanesfarm.org

Riggin' Up an Outpost Bathtub

Time: approximately 1 hour
Skill Level: beginner–intermediate

Supplies and Tools:
6   12" x 12" concrete pavers
5' cast-iron tub
2-burner propane camp stove
6' (or more) flexible gas line
5-gallon propane bottle with regulator
Crescent wrench

Instructions:
1. Lay concrete pavers on a level, undisturbed 2' x 3' piece of ground.
2. Position your tub on top of the pavers and your camp stove underneath the tub.
3. Attach the gas line to the propane stove on one end and the propane bottle on other end. (If you decide to hide the propane tank, you can build a small wooden box around it. Make sure the box you build has a couple of air vents in the sides.)
4. If the area where you're situating your bathtub is prone to wind, you can do one of two things: build an unmortared brick wall around the tub on three sides with numerous gaps for air flow, or build a skirt around the tub on three sides out of metal flashing. Either way, be sure to leave gaps large enough to allow access to valves for lighting and regulation.

Find embroidery instructions and more in *MaryJane's Stitching Room*, www.maryjanesfarm.org

Wall Tent Getaways

The very best place to put your outpost bathtub is next to a wall tent. On occasion, when I use the words "wall tent," the phrase draws a blank look. A wall tent is more than just a tent—it can be a tiny home away from home: four walls and sometimes running water, or in my case, a luxurious bed, woodstove, and bathtub. If you have access to a little bit of land or even a city rooftop, you can satisfy your "cabin escape" fantasy in no time at all and for very little money by creating a "wall tent" retreat, complete with a bathtub out back.

When I was working for the Forest Service, living thirty miles from road's end in a canvas wall tent in the dead of winter, I never dreamed I would someday be the owner of five tents for rent—the only wall tent B&B ever featured in the *New York Times Magazine*.

My wall tents are secluded, nestled throughout my orchard, each with a salvaged barn-wood floor and a full antique iron bed blanketed in organic sheets and piled high with goose-down pillows and comforters. The tents are lit with oil lanterns and warmed by wood-burning stoves that can also be used for cooking. Each tent has a front and rear deck for enjoying a good book or bath to the chorus of crickets and coyotes, and a fully functional outdoor kitchen with a propane stove, cold-water sink, and campfire.

It's really my version of an "organic safari." Guests go "hunting" around my farm for things like fruit, eggs, and berries. Surrounded by hay fields, fruit trees, and gardens for nibbling in, it's a luxurious getaway. A communal organic breakfast featuring our own eggs, fruits, and vegetables is served around a campfire every morning. You just can't beat the romance and aroma of coffee percolating on a morning campfire.

Guests use our environmentally friendly outhouses and showerhouses, but the feature they love the most are my outdoor bathtubs, as seen on the previous page.

For more details about how to create your own wall tent getaway, my first book, *MaryJane's Ideabook, Cookbook, Lifebook*, has blueprints and more. The Web provides a wealth of resources for back-to-nature getaways similar to mine, but the very best will be the one you call your own.

Up On the Roof

"A certain thrill comes from sleeping and showering outside with the skyline as my wallpaper. It allows me to engage with the city in a special way," says New York City architect Ross Anderson.

When Anderson moved his firm to the top floor of a New York City building several years ago, he didn't hesitate to claim his escape. Anderson transformed the building's tar roof into an urban campground outfitted with a wall tent, an outdoor shower, and other amenities. To facilitate easy access to the roof, the architect cut a hole in the ceiling of his office and installed a new "stairway to heaven." Open skies are now just a few steps away from the drafting tables of Anderson Architects.

Ross' rooftop escape is utilized by his staff for breaks, meetings, and parties. Occasionally, when Ross is working late, he spends the night. "When I'm in bed and the canvas tent flap is snapping in the wind, I feel like I've been transported to a wonderful place far away."

DEAR FARMSTAY GUEST
IN AN EFFORT TO CONSERVE WATER
PLEASE SELECT A TOWEL AND
MARK IT WITH A LAUNDRY
NUMBER, THEN HANG YOUR
PERSONALIZED TOWEL
OUTSIDE ON THE LINE TO DRY

THANKS
MARY JANES FARM

Tip: **Duds to Suds**

Don't toss those little bits of leftover soap pieces. Put them in a blender with water. Voilà! Liquid soap ready for your hand-pump soap dispenser. Or toss them into the toes of a nylon stocking that you keep knotted around your showerhead. Just grab the end and lather away. Give guests their very own fresh bar of soap by cutting full-size bars into smaller slices and then wrapping them in pretty bits of fabric scraps or odds and ends of twill tape or ribbon.

OUTPOST LIGHTING

It took me a few years to get my outpost candle lighting just right. I tried candles placed in shallow jars, but the wind still blew them out. If I put a candle inside a tall bottle protected from the wind, it was hard to light and the candle was difficult to replace. My idea here solves all those problems. You can access the candle from below, and it stays where you put it because you've pushed it down onto a screw. My lanterns can swing from trees in a windstorm and stay lit. Not to mention, they're fun to embellish.

Make an Outpost Lantern

Time: approximately 1 hour
Skill Level: beginner–intermediate

Materials and Tools:
2   jars
Bottle cutter (I use the QuickSilver Bottle Cutter, www.khue.com)
"Duco Cement" glue
Clamp
Drill
1" screw
20-gauge wire
Lace (optional)

Instructions:
1. Using a bottle cutter, cut the bottoms off of two jars.
2. Place one jar top down and apply glue to the cut edge. Carefully set the second jar on the first, cut edges together. Place a small piece of wood on top of the jars and gently clamp until the glue has dried thoroughly.
3. Drill or punch a hole in the center of the bottom lid; insert a screw for holding the candle in place. For the top of the lantern, use only the threaded portion of the lid to allow for air circulation. In the rim of this lid, drill holes for mounting your lantern hanger. Make and attach a wire hanger, using the photo as a guide.
4. Glue lace around jar seam if desired. Place candle on bottom lid and screw it down firmly. Screw lid to base of jar lantern.

For added flair, attach chandelier crystals to the base lid, and substitute a vintage necklace for the wire hanger (make sure the necklace is strong enough to support the weight of the lantern!).

Make vintage enamelware cups into outdoorsy candles for use inside your wall tent using melted wax and a wick (beeswax is my favorite because of its luscious fragrance).

OUTPOST PLANTS

Container gardening can turn any outdoor space, no matter how urban or small, into an outpost. Crocks, wagons, bowls, and even old boots full of green life bring us closer to nature. Being close to "wild" things has the power to revive us, and flowering plants fill an outpost with color and fragrance, known to inspire romance, playfulness, and creativity.

Begonias are my outpost plant of choice. Seeing their luscious but delicate blooms buoys my spirit. I've tried many shade-loving container plants, but when it was all said and done, begonias performed the best. They're easy to care for and don't need a lot of water. With just a little nurturing, begonias offer gorgeous blooms throughout the summer, up until the first frost.

There are lots of begonia species out there. Some types are annuals; others are perennial. Some are evergreen, some deciduous. They come in climbing, trailing, shrub, and succulent varieties. This incredible diversity means you can easily find a begonia to suit your growing conditions and skill level.

I grow my outdoor begonias as perennials, bringing the tubers indoors from season to season. When it's time for them to hibernate, I remove them from their containers, gently brush most of the dirt off, and let them dry in paper sacks in my kitchen. Then I over-winter them in my pumphouse in a basket because it's moist, cool, and dark there, but never drops below freezing. The ideal storage temperature range is 40–50°F, so an unheated attic, basement, or three-season porch would also work.

The tender tubers shouldn't be planted outdoors until after the last chance of frost, but they can be started indoors four weeks beforehand. Fill flats or pots with potting mixtures that offer good drainage. Place each tuber hollow-side-up under about a half inch of soil, water them once really well to wake them up, and place them in a warm, bright spot. Unless the soil gets very dry, don't water again until you see some growth. You can expect to see shoots coming up in about a month.

During the weeks you're waiting for your begonia babies to sprout, you'll have time to imagine your green retreat. Visualize your outpost in bloom. Do you see an eclectic collection of pots and baskets brimming with blossoms? A trellised climber adorning an outpost bed? Or maybe a simple flower box along the length of a porch railing? Trim and tidy or unruly and wild—you get to start over every year and have it your way.

Hens and Chicks, drought-tolerant succulents, are some of my favorite plants to grow in worn-out boots. Once you get them started, they'll last for years without needing any attention. Their genus, *Sempervivum*, is Latin for "always live" and their species, *tectorum*, means "on roofs." It turns out that Hens and Chicks were traditionally planted on European thatched roofs. According to folklore, it was thought they would provide protection against lightning-induced fires because the plant held sway with the gods of lightning, Thor and Zeus. Folklore aside, Hens and Chicks are "succulents," which store water in their leaves and stems, making them naturally fire-resistant.

Snapdragons do well in wagons as long as the wagon has a few rusty holes in the bottom for drainage. Your moveable garden can be outside decorating your "outpost" one day and then inside decorating your kitchen the next. Think "vessel" everywhere you go and you'll be surprised how many you'll find. Flowers and vines spilling from old wire colanders, farm buckets, wagons, wooden crates, bins—even upside-down old straw hats—make good vessels for your outpost plants.

Outpost Plants Indoors

Sustainable landscaping isn't an expanse of perfect lawn meticulously fertilized and watered on schedule. It means seeking out and planting drought-resistant plants, preferably native plants. It means rethinking the way water is used and lessening the amount required. It means wild and native, pure and simple.

Where I live, it specifically means "bringing back the pure Palouse prairie," the two-million-acre region where I live. The Palouse is noted for the remarkable and uniquely fertile soils deposited there by wind—much in the same way sand dunes are formed in the Sahara Desert—with waves of black, rich topsoil that are twelve feet deep in places.

My neighbor, Jacie Jensen, whose farm borders mine to the west, recognized early on that the hundred acres she and her husband steward near the top of Paradise Ridge was home to historic and rare plants—perhaps one of the last remaining examples of pure Palouse prairie to be found. Over the past 120 years, the advent of agriculture has reshaped the Palouse region from the short-grass prairie it once was into the monoculture landscape we see today.

Jacie knew that the establishment of drought-resistant and sustainable landscapes depended on the availability of seeds from the native wildflowers and grass species she found growing on her little piece of paradise. She began an ambitious and difficult undertaking: the labor-intensive task of walking the ridge repeatedly with a sack on her back collecting seeds. In order to avoid continuous seed mining of the few survivors remaining, she eventually figured out how to grow them in "seed-increase plots." She uses seeds from the plots to grow flats of her wild grasses and flowers in a commercial greenhouse, marketing them as "Palouse Prairie in a Flat" under her new company name, Thorn Creek Native Seed Farm.

Jacie is yet another example of the women nationwide who play a role in figuring out how to embrace our ancient wild landscapes for the benefit of future generations.

Grow Wild to Know Wild

The time has finally arrived. With more and more seed companies teaming up with native plant societies and "running wild"—offering exotic and indigenous native grasses and wildflowers for sale—we can get involved in something bigger than ourselves when we take to our gardens. When you grow native, you're keeping some plants from going extinct. And native plants tend to be much more drought tolerant than traditional nursery fare. Once you get them started, they're easy to grow.

Because I wanted to truly "know" what was once native to my backyard, I decided to grow them in glass vases first. Not only would they have a classy-looking home, I'd be able to check out their root growth on a daily basis. Because the glass vases I chose didn't have drainage holes, I put four inches of washed 1/8-inch gravel in first, then a square of paper towel (to keep the soil from washing into the gravel), and lastly, some native soil. It's easy to overwater plants grown in a vase without drainage holes, but since mine were in glass, I could see clearly how much water they had access to.

When I felt like the plants had outgrown their vessels, I planted them outside where they belong, but after fussing indoors with my native plants over the course of a season, I feel more intimate with the wild outside my door.

OUTSPOKEN...
Right-to-dry Activists
Prefer Airing Their Laundry in Public

Who would ever imagine that drying clothing outdoors with the sun and wind could be illegal?

Yet unbelievably, homeowner associations prohibit or restrict outdoor clotheslines in an estimated sixty million American yards, says Alexander Lee, founder of the organization Project Laundry List (www.laundrylist.org). Lee launched Project Laundry List in 1995 after hearing Helen Caldicott, the Australian anti-nuclear activist, suggest energy-saving alternatives like drying clothes outdoors.

Electric dryers use more energy than almost any other household appliances, consuming the rough equivalent of thirty million tons of coal each year in the U.S. alone. However, since 1999, Utah and Florida have passed right-to-dry laws, and pressure is now mounting in California, where an estimated seven million households have clothesline restrictions, Lee says.

Clothesline supporters like Lee say hanging clothes offers rewards beyond energy savings. "I don't want to sound preachy," he says, "but it's so easy and so beautiful. It's art."

" *Congratulations!* " says the message attached to a package of clothespins.

" *You are being a smart eco-citizen* by hanging your laundry outside to dry. "

50

OUTSPOKEN...
Backyard Outlaws

Taylor Valliant (my former assistant graphics designer) claims her love of chickens started here at my farm. But little did she know when she hit the open road for Montana, her free-range days were numbered ...

"It's a silly law, and something needs to be done about it,"

Morgan says. "If we want people to eat locally, be less dependent on food that comes from who knows where, we ought to do something about it."

When Taylor Valliant moved to Missoula, Montana, with her husband Morgan, they became outlaws. Their crime? Raising backyard chickens.

"We are interested in sustainability and raising food," Morgan explained. "We've just had a baby, and we're interested in raising him to understand where food comes from. It's important to do that."

Unfortunately the Missoula rule is no chickens, even if your neighbors love them. "It's a silly law, and something needs to be done about it," Morgan said. "If we want people to eat locally, be less dependent on food that comes from who knows where, we ought to do something about it."

Missoula's mayor, John Engen, agrees. "It seems that if we want to be a town that does its part for sustainability, this is something we ought to consider. I think we want to allow folks to use their good judgment and move toward more sustainable food practices."

That's precisely the sentiment that Taylor and Morgan hope will carry the day.

"We don't think we're going to change the world by having a few chickens, but it's still important when we talk about where our food comes from. It's important on a personal level and a collective level," said Taylor. "If we had a half-dozen chickens, we would be able to keep the neighbors in eggs. That would be neighborly, and that seems like what we want our town to be about."

For compact backyard chicken and rabbit houses, see www.omlet.co.uk.

NATURALLY
Gifted

Outdoorsy Gifts for the People on Your List

For a keeper of memories, a "gathering bottle" full of collected stones becomes a photo display gift when adorned with a cork, a bit of lace, some 26-gauge wire attached to a clothespin, and 16-gauge wire curlicues.

Vintage flower frogs are a unique way to give the gift of photos.

Don't get hung up on how to create this exact candle holder—just take the supplies listed here and start twisting wire until you come up with your own unique design. Once the metal lathe is wrapped around your jar, all else attaches easily to it.

1 Wide-mouth Quart Jar
1 Large Candle (to fit inside your jar)
4 Small Votive Candles
Wire, 16 and 20 gauge
Diamond-mesh Metal Lathe (enough to go around your jar with a 1/2" overlap)
4 Fishing Trollers
1 Fishing Lure
Beads (to cover the barbed hooks)

The exquisite "lures of the past" artwork adorning this pack of playing cards was created by Jon Q Wright (www.jqoutdoors.com), recognized worldwide for his spectacular paintings and illustrations of wildlife and nature scenes. Find these and other "gifts for the outdoor enthusiast" at www.riversedgeproducts.com .

Fifties-style silverware with detachable handles can be easily found in thrift stores. Using pliers, loosen and discard the original plastic handles (or find another use for them). Select branches to match the size of the silverware. Cut to desired length. Sand the edges. Drill a hole the size of the stem of your utensil end. Glue in place and let dry.

Hand-crafted twig letters that speak to the heart are easy to make. They can mount on any wall or rest in a window sill. Besides names, create words like DREAM, WILD, LAUGH, and HOME.

Using a pair of common garden snips, bring home an array of green twigs at least 1/4-inch in diameter. As you design your letters, cut and sand each piece. Once you have them all laid out, take 26-gauge wire and 1/2-inch finish nails and start putting them together, gently tapping the nails into the ends and then wrapping with wire to reinforce (raffia and string also work, or a combination of all four as shown here). Adorn with treasures found in nature and 16-gauge wire curlicues poked into the ends.

NO *Child* LEFT INSIDE!

> " If I ever needed another testament to tell me that people thrive in the outdoors, all I need to do is take my little one outside. She loves it! If she is crying or fussing or overly tired, she immediately quiets when we go outside. She eats better and goes into her quiet alert stage (which is when they do the most learning) almost immediately. Of course, I try to avoid the hottest part of the day, but it is so much fun to watch her learning about the world when we take walks in the morning and evening. Or even just when we change the sprinkler around or let the dog out. "

Elizaray,
from "MaryJane's Outpost Dispatch"
www.maryjanesoutpost.org

> " If someone said, 'Write a sentence about your life,' I'd write, 'I want to *go outside and play.*' "
> – Jenna Elfman, Golden Globe recipient

Children and the outdoors seem like a "natural" fit, don't they? But the Mayberry scene I grew up in is in short supply these days, so I've been on a mission to come up with innovative ideas to get kids out the door. I figure if I can get women revved up, any kids involved will follow in their footsteps.

One way is to model nature-friendly behaviors that our kids can emulate. Here's a good example. My daughter (at age twenty) said, "I should thank you for teaching me never to complain about the weather. One of my friends comments about it constantly in a negative way. It's either too hot or too cold, too rainy, too snowy … grumble, grumble. It seems so odd to me, and I realize that's because I've never once heard you complain about the weather— and you're a farmer! Consequently, Momma, it's my habit as well, to never *not* like the weather."

Yup, weather is weather. I got that trait from my parents and passed it along effortlessly. It's the perfect example of how outlook is everything. Like so many things in life, weather is completely outside our control, so why bother being negative about it? If it's raining, think Gene Kelly. Take off your shoes and dance. If it's hot, think detox. Nothing does the trick better than a good sweat. (I grew up in Utah before air conditioning.) If it's cold, think cozy and bundled up. Make a vow, right now, never to complain about the weather again, especially in front of children. It's a simple thing, but it will have a huge impact. The weather will be the weather, whether or not you complain, so embrace it. Make the best of it … then get out in it!

"Clean enuf to be healthy, but dirty enuf to be happy!"

Letting Nature Nurture

Close your eyes and think back to the summers of your childhood. Maybe you remember running through the sun-bright shower of a garden sprinkler, collecting rocks, climbing trees, or just lying on your back watching clouds mosey across blue sky. Those were the days when goals were simple: how fast can I pedal my bike? And pleasures were as pure as dewdrops on morning grass.

Now, take a minute to consider how much time kids these days spend outdoors. Pales in comparison, doesn't it? Today, it seems schedules often get in the way of play, and outside time gets sacrificed for all of those "important" tasks on our to-do lists. Kids are becoming more and more busy, rushing through meals to get to the next scheduled thing. Worse yet, they're "plugging in" to electronic devices during their downtime. With so much hustle and bustle, nature gets tuned out, and the side effects are not only unfortunate, they're downright unhealthy.

Research is providing us with strong reasons to rearrange our priorities and "schedule" wild time for our children. A study by the Kaiser Family Foundation found that the average American child spends forty-four hours a week staring at television and computer screens—that's more than six hours a day! Similar studies link this kind of electronic excess to a nasty list of child health risks generally associated with soaring stress levels, including: obesity, violence, ADD (and ADHD), and decreased immunity. Kids' senses are being overwhelmed and ultimately desensitized by so much technological stimulation.

Richard Louv, chairman of the Children & Nature Network and author of the 2005 book *Last Child in the Woods*, has dubbed the disconnection between kids and the outdoors "nature deficit disorder." One of the primary symptoms of this condition is the substitution of screen time for green time. According to Louv, the way children understand and experience their neighborhoods and the natural world has changed radically in the past few decades. Even as they become better educated about conserving the natural environment, their actual physical contact with it is fading—and their health is suffering as a result.

" I went out for a walk and finally concluded to stay out till sundown, for

going out, I found, was really going in. "

– John Muir

The National Wildlife Federation recommends that

parents provide their kids with one "green hour" every day

in order to establish (or restore) their relationship with the natural world.

Is there a bright side to all of this? You bet. The same studies that show us why our kids are in jeopardy also tell us how we can fix it. The remedy is as simple as stepping out the door.

Kids need enough time outside to muddle through that initial "I'm bored" feeling. When left to their own devices, they will find their way to curiosity, imagination, and awe—tools that we humans need in order to live full, rich lives. The National Wildlife Federation's Green Hour Program, www.greenhour.org, recommends that parents provide their kids with one "green hour" every day in order to establish (or restore) their relationship with the natural world. This means at least one hour of unfettered play outside. It doesn't matter if it takes place in the backyard or the backcountry—the benefits are the same. Kids who spend time outside will instantly feel more relaxed and creative, and the good vibes will translate into conscientious attitudes toward themselves, others, and the world around them.

If a green hour seems tough to come by, then sit down and jot your schedule on paper. Seeing it in black and white can make it easier to find spots where you can tighten up and "schedule" free time outside.

Live and Learn Together

Okay, so you've done it—you've wrangled your youngster out the door. Now what? Baby steps, literally. Don't fret, pressure, or rush. Just start wandering. Let your feet take you where they will, and make lots of stops along the way to smell, hear, feel, and look at things around you. Observe birds overhead, listen to their songs. Touch the bark of trees and note their differences. Smell leaves, watch for animal tracks, and talk about what busy insects might be doing on their travels. These are the little things, and these are the things that matter.

If you find yourself getting impatient with your child's pace, temper your urge to hurry them along by taking a more active lead in your excursions. Plan some activities to do together. Structured exploration can offer you a chance to bond, teach, and learn with your child, keeping things interesting for both of you.

The Vermont Institute of Natural Science has published two books that will give you all the inspiration and how-to instruction you need. *Small Wonders: Nature Education for Young Children*, by Linda Garrett and Hannah Thomas, is a nature curriculum designed for parents and educators of young children (ages three to six). Twenty-four exploration units encourage hands-on learning about growth and change, animal homes, and connections to nature. Whether it's counting flower petals or singing about habitats, you can help your little one practice important skills like observing, sorting, predicting, and following directions.

For older kids, pick up *Hands-On Nature: Information and Activities for Exploring the Environment with Children,* by Susan Sawyer, Jenepher Lingelbach, and Lisa Purcell. In this book, forty field-tested, experiential activities explore five themes: Adaptations, Habitats, Cycles, Designs of Nature, and Earth and Sky. They're easy to set up and follow, and several of the units include puppet-show scripts and games to lighten up the lessons.

Backyard Getaways

Once your family gets in touch with nature, the call of the wild might beckon you farther off the beaten path. If you're intimidated by the thought of "roughing it" with the kids, practice on a small scale. Pitch a tent in the backyard, cook on a camp stove, and play outdoors for a night. From there, you can progress to a weekend camping trip closer to home.

Rebekah Teal is a lawyer and former judge who lives in the "wilderness" of a large metropolitan area. She and her six-year-old daughter have learned to experience the wilderness in their very own backyard.

"It all started when I made a concerted effort to be more outdoorsy," explains Rebekah. "I upped 'get in touch with nature' on my priority list. I decided to experience the great outdoors at night, all night. But I didn't want to be in the actual wilderness. I'm not *that* outdoorsy."

So Rebekah decided to spend a night outside under the stars in her backyard. She invited both her daughter and her husband to join her. Her husband, a successful venture capitalist, laughed and said, "No way," but her daughter jumped up and down with excitement.

The preparations for a backyard campout are different from those for a wilderness campout. Rebekah's only preparations for her backyard adventure were to clear a place in the yard for a campfire, get some firewood, bring out their sleeping bags and pillows, and find the marshmallows.

That first night out under the stars in the backyard wasn't perfect, but it was still magical, she said. "I was quite uncomfortable that first night. I loved being outside, but the thought of snakes, mosquitoes, spiders, and criminals put me on edge. I couldn't sleep in a sleeping bag on the ground, and I was shocked at how noisy it was in our yard at night. Add all that together and you've got a sleepless night," she said. "But it made this all the more of an adventure, and my daughter loved it."

The first thing Rebekah did after that first sleepless night was to buy a pup tent. She spent less than twenty dollars on the tent she calls "cramped, yet cozy." "That little tent gives me the peace of mind I need to close my eyes and fall asleep outside. It's also so small that it's a breeze to set up and take down."

> " It is good to realize that if love and peace can prevail on earth, *and if we can teach our children to honor nature's gifts,* the joys and beauties of the outdoors will be here forever. "
>
> – Jimmy Carter

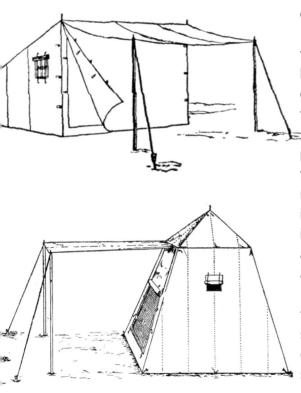

> *" So far, the best part is cooking eggs over a campfire and looking at planets. "*
> – six-year-old Alyssa Teal

There goes the neighborhood!

Rebekah also learned to take a sound machine with her to block out the noise of suburbia. "The sound machine is necessary where we live. It's just too noisy outside at night to sleep. Our favorite selection for background sound is a 'mountain brook.' We gaze at the actual night sky and listen to a virtual brook." Now Rebekah and her daughter camp in their backyard at least once a month.

Getting close to nature is not the easiest thing to do in suburbia. Rebekah believes that spending nights outdoors is vital and renewing. "Being outside at night is different than being outside during the day. It is far more intense. In our area, like many others, almost every tree has been ripped up to make way for development. Nature is hard to find sometimes. Our backyard campouts are easy, quick, and fun. They help us develop a love of, a respect for, and a closeness to nature. There's no denying it, there's something deeply renewing about falling asleep outside under the moon and stars."

> 66 *There they stand,*
> the innumerable stars,
> shining in order like a living hymn,
> written in light. 99
> – N. P. Willis

GAMES

Copy Me: It's fun to play a game of "Copy Me"! Have kids lay on their backs and kick like a roach ... or on all fours like a lion and "growl" ... or paw like a kitten ... or slither like snakes on their tummies. I run a daycare and this is the technique I use when I need little ones to stay in one place and be quiet: "Snakes can't talk, they can only *sssssss*," keeps them occupied and quiet for a little while. If you have older kids around, let them take turns picking animals.

Water Balloons: Fill small water balloons and lay them in the grass like easter eggs. When someone says "Go!" kids run to pick up the ballons and throw them at a picture of a funny face tacked to a tree. That way, the kids don't throw the balloons at each other, but they get to run, throw, compete, and get something wet!

– Heather, MaryJane's Farmgirl Connection, www.maryjanesfarm.org

STARGAZING

When you blaze a trail far from the lights of civilization, the night sky will reward you. In town, it's easy to forget just how many minuscule points of light we can't see. A friend of mine told me that the first time her son saw the Milky Way while camping, he exclaimed, "Momma, it's a snowstorm way up in the sky!"

Kids love stories about stars and constellations (named groups of stars like Pegasus, below). They'll be riveted by the accompanying myths and facts like:

• Stars in a constellation may appear close to one another, but they can be hundreds of light years apart, and one light year equals about six thousand billion miles!

• Even though we draw stars with points and imagine them in the night sky that way, they only seem to have points because they twinkle. They twinkle because we see them through the air, which contains tiny droplets of water.

Two handy tools to have at camp are a star-watching field guide and a planisphere. A planisphere a is a circular star chart that can be adjusted to show the starscape for any latitude, time, and date. A variety of field guides and planispheres are available from Acorn Naturalists (www.acornnaturalists.com).

Carpe Noctem—Seize the Night!

Not so long ago, you could drive a few miles out of town after dark and find nighttime as nature intended it. Silent shadows draped the landscape, and a black canopy of limitless stars arched overhead. Stargazing was the kind of experience that inspired wonder, providing people with a healthy sense of smallness in a universe so grand.

Now, with so many Americans living in artificially lit urban areas, we're actually facing a crisis of light pollution. Half of our country's children have never even seen the Milky Way! Sadly, when they look up at the night sky, they only see a gray haze that astronomers call "sky glow."

Light pollution, according to the astronomers at the International Dark-Sky Association (IDA), has far-reaching adverse effects on air and water quality, human health, wildlife populations, and cultural integrity. The IDA strives to conserve our precious darkness by raising awareness of light pollution and educating people about better options in outdoor lighting. To learn more about how you can combat light pollution, visit the International Dark-Sky Association at www.darksky.org.

Pegasus

STORY TREE

*An' all us children,
when the supper things was done,
we ran to the Story Tree
to dream who we'd become.*

– Anonymous

The best gift we can give our children is also one of the simplest: the gift of reading. It's cheap entertainment, and if there's a library nearby, it's not only cheap, it's free. Books are such a basic commodity these days, they're often taken for granted. Yet the results of reading with a child are infinitely rewarding.

Within a week of my granddaughter's birth, my daughter and son-in-law began reading to her as a nightly bedtime ritual. As a result, before she could even talk, she would hold her dolls in her lap and read to them in a language only she and her dolly understood. She carried books around the house, she laid her head on them, she cradled them. She was immersed in books, a world full of secrets yet to be discovered.

It's easy to instill a love of books in a child. We don't have to wait until kids "understand" each and every word to begin reading to them. To be successful in school, it is estimated that a child needs to know close to five thousand words before she enters kindergarten. I used to read my own adult books to my infant children. Infants love hearing the animated rhythm and melody of your voice. It helps them develop keen listening skills. And at just a few months of age, when a little one can point to pictures on a page, speaking the names of familiar objects will impart the importance of language before the written word is even realized. And if you prefer spinning a yarn off the top of your head, storytelling is every bit as inspiring.

Although the lives of parents are often hectic, schedule a specific time each day to read to your child. Don't be discouraged if you end up skipping a day or don't always stick to your schedule; just don't give up.

Reading aloud to your child on a daily basis not only sows the seeds of a lush vocabulary, it also stimulates her imagination and expands her understanding of the world. This vital skill can equip kids with the inclination to seek wholesome solace and stimulation in the pages of a good book when they're feeling bored, overwhelmed, or blue. Literary journeys give all of us an immediate escape from everyday cares, and we discover empathy for all walks of life along the way—precious gifts every child deserves. Remember, you are your child's first teacher. All it takes is a story.

Growing Dreams

Given my passionate love of reading, I was asked to participate in an early childhood initiative designed to help children from birth to age six experience books. KHQ Spokane's "Success by Six" campaign creates short 30-second TV spots featuring well-known people encouraging parents to read to their children. For my TV spot, I was sitting on the porch of my little bunkhouse reading to my granddaughter and her friend. The book I chose to read was *Growing Seasons,* the story of four girls who grew up on a turn-of-the-century farm. Not only do I want to see more books in the hands of children, I hope to inspire more young girls to become farmers when they grow up. I know I'm doing my job because I heard one of the four-year-old girls who comes to my farm frequently tell a little boy who said he wanted to be a farmer when he grew up, "You have to be a *girl* to be a farmer."

My Garden

By MAURICE HILL

I'm plant-ing dai-sies, plant-ing pinks in half a doz-en rows, I'm plant-ing stocks and mar-i-golds. Each day my gar-den grows! My flow-ers al-ways are in bloom, but if you were to look, you'd be sur-prised to find my gar-den past-ed in a book.

"... you'd be surprised to find my garden pasted in a book!"

My collection of vintage scrapbooks created by children, including the one put together by my mother-in-law when she was a young 'un, is an absolute treasure. Long before scrapbooking became a billion-dollar industry, it was a common pastime for children. Garden scrapbooks are worth reviving because discarded magazines are everywhere! It's a simple hobby. All you need to get your child started is a good pair of scissors (blunt-tipped if they're too young for pointed), a blank book, and some glue. Here's an entry from Ruth's, my mother-in-law. I can't do her entire book justice here, but the "clip art" in her book has been of value to my designers repeatedly for brochures and more. So, help your child create a family heirloom by letting them clip out photos or drawings of veggies, flowers, and barnyard critters. Cut and paste, old-timey style!

Rig Up a Tree Swing

There's no simpler pleasure than soaring to the skies on a tree swing. How else can you have your head in the clouds and still tickle your toes in the grass? A tree swing is fun and easy to rig up, and it is guaranteed to incite endless squeals of delight from "kids" of all ages.

Materials and Tools You'll Need:

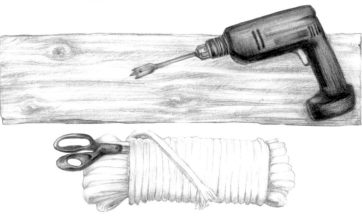

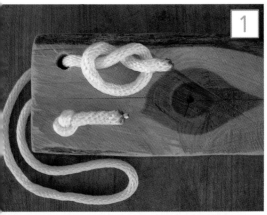

- A good, sturdy tree limb
- One cedar board for your seat (cedar is weather resistant). It should be at least 20" long, 6" wide, and 1 1/2" thick. If you're buying from a hardware store, you can have a board cut to size.
- 60-grit sandpaper
- About 75 feet of 3/4" braided nylon rope (more or less depending on the height of your tree limb). You can use a natural fiber like manila, but nylon will be more weather- and wear-resistant.
- Scissors or knife
- Matches or lighter
- T-square or ruler and pencil
- Drill with a 3/4" boring bit
- Hammer and 4 fence staples or bent nails
- About 10' of twine (optional)

Here's How You Do It:

1. **Measure** and **mark** spots for holes at each corner of your board. The center of each hole should be at least 1 1/2" from the edges of the board.

2. **Drill** each hole about 3/4 of the way through the board (so that you can just see the drill-bit tip sticking through the bottom). Flip the board over and finish drilling the holes to prevent the wood from splitting.

3. **Sand** any rough spots, including corners and edges.

4. **Cut** two 4' lengths of rope. Use a match or lighter to melt the ends a bit to prevent unraveling.

5. **Thread** the ends of one rope through the holes on one side of the board. **Tie** granny knots (photo 1) in each end, then fold the tails over and **secure** them to the board with a fence staple or bent nail. Repeat on the opposite end of the board.

6. Take the rest of your rope and **tie** a figure-8 loop knot (photo 2) in the end. **Toss** the knotted end up and over your tree branch (it helps to secure a weight to the end, but be careful not to let it come down on your head!).

7. **Shimmy** the rope around on the limb until it is positioned about 2' out and away from the tree trunk.

8. Hold the knotted end of the rope and **thread** the other end all the way through the loop in the knot. **Pull** until the knot cinches snug against the underside of the tree limb (photo 3).

9. **Cut** the rope off about a foot above ground level. This will give you plenty of rope to work with when tying on the seat.

10. **Repeat** steps 6 through 9 with the remaining length of rope, except this time shimmy the rope about 2' out on the limb from your first knot. Also, make sure your knots line up well on the limb. Now, you have two ropes hanging from the limb.

11. **Tie** the hanging ends to the loops on the swing seat using becket bend knots (photos 4 and 5), making sure your seat is level. The swing seat should hang high enough that your child can touch the ground with the balls of her feet but not her heels. The becket bend is a great knot because it's both strong and adjustable.

12. As a finishing touch, you can **wrap** a 2' length of twine around the becket bend knots and the loose ends of rope.

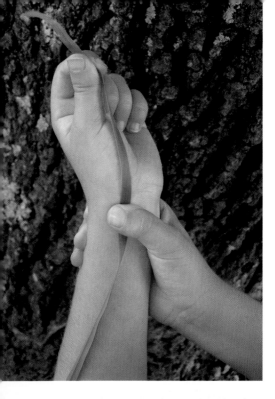

GRASS WHISTLING

The glorious squawk of a grass whistle is one of the most giggle-icious sounds you'll ever hear in the great Outdoors, and anybody who can pick a blade of grass can do it. Here's how:

1. Pick a thick piece of grass that's about 6–8" long.
2. Pinch the grass with the thumb and index finger of the left hand.
3. Keeping the grass smooth and tight, press the right thumb against the left.
4. There will be a little hole between your thumbs that is divided by the grass blade.
5. Press your lips against the hole, blow good and hard, and get ready for giggles. You'll be amazed how loud you can honk!

You stay here. I'll whistle if it's safe to follow me.

What will you do if it isn't safe?

Scream!

– Terry Pratchett

TWO-HANDED WHISTLING

Hand whistling, or "cooing," is pure old-fashioned fun. The concept is simple: Cup both hands tightly with your thumbs together, and blow through your thumbs. Much like blowing into a bottle, the air resonates inside the hands and flows out, creating a sound similar to the cooing of a dove. It takes some practice to master the technique, but once you get good at it, you can whistle anything from owl calls to Dixie. Here's how:

1. Lay the outer edge of your left hand against the base of the fingers on your right hand (reverse hands if you're a lefty).
2. Cup your hands together so that the fingers of the left hand press into the right hand between the index finger and the thumb. Try to form an air-tight seal.
3. Bend the thumbs and bring them together so there's an opening between them about the size of a keyhole.
4. Press your lips against your thumb knuckles and blow with moderate force. You should feel the air blowing out the thumb "keyhole" beneath your bottom lip.
5. Keep adjusting your fingers and thumbs until you start to hear a whistle. It may be faint at first, but it will become clearer in no time. Experiment with blowing harder or squeezing your hands tighter for higher notes, blowing softer and relaxing for lower notes. You can also try bending your fingers more or less in order to control the note even more.

ANIMAL SHADOWS

Dog

Rabbit

Kangaroo

Baby Birds

All you need is a sunlit sheet by day or a lantern-lit wall by night, and you have a hand shadow theater waiting to happen.

Find a "screen" for your theater. A tent wall, light-colored sheet, piece of paper, or bedroom wall will work fine (the whiter the surface and brighter the light, the sharper the shadow images will be). If you're relying on sunlight, make sure it's shining directly onto your surface so that your hands will cast shadows. A flashlight can be positioned as needed. (Tip: A bright flickering candle makes shadows dance!)

Take turns with your kids trying these hand shadows, or make up your own. Ask them if they can figure out how to make their shadows smaller and larger. Can they touch shadows without touching hands? Can they make their shadows move and "talk"? Kids will get a kick out of making their own shadow movie starring handmade creatures of all kinds.

Rooster

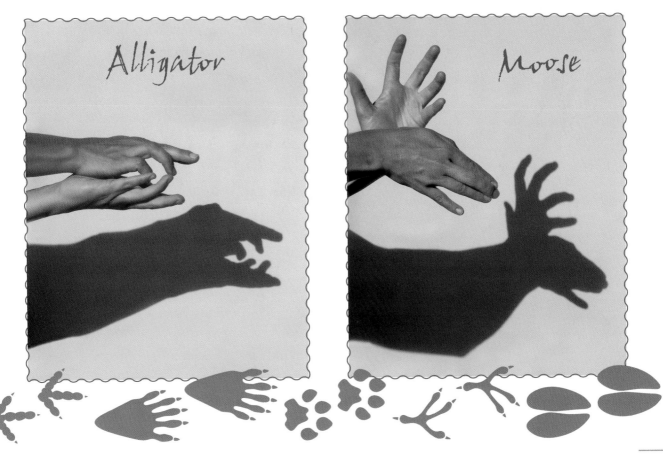

Alligator

Moose

Build a Backyard Lean-to

A lean-to is an easy backyard playhouse that promises hours of imaginative play. Kids love building things—especially things they can crawl into and call their own—so they'll be gung-ho to help haul sticks. And when they see their efforts taking shape, they'll instantly start planning a fort, an Indian camp, or a summer sun-tea party!

Materials and Tools You'll Need:

- Seven sturdy stick poles that are 8–10' long
- Rope or twine
- Scissors or knife
- Lots of branches that are 6–10' long (it's okay if leaves are still attached; they'll help cover your lean-to and add camouflage).

Here's How You Do It:

1. Find two trees that are 6–8' apart, and lash one sturdy pole between them horizontally. It can be anywhere from 3–5' above the ground. Wrap your twine around the tree and pole ends several times and tie securely.

2. Lean the rest of the poles against the cross pole at about a sixty degree angle and about a foot apart.

3. Starting at one side of the cross pole, wrap a length of twine around each pole, securing it to the cross pole, and tie off at the other end.

4. Pile branches on top of your poles, from the ground up, to create your roof. Lash them to the vertical poles. Keep piling and lashing branches until you reach the top. Holes between branches can be filled with leaves and grass, or left open for "windows."

5. You can add more branches to the sides or front of the lean-to for a more secret hideaway.

6. Finally, decorate with flowers, fabric, paint, antlers, or garland—anything goes!

THE ART OF
Outside Rituals

Helen and Allen Butters, 1943

"Hon?" I heard my parents say in an asking voice at least once a day. "Hon" (or sometimes "Sweetie" or "Sugar") was how they invited each other to tea every day for some sixty years. "Hon" meant, "I'm ready, are you?"

Tea in the winter involved filling their Jewel Tea Aladdin-style teapot with hot water, poured through the built-in tea strainer that was part of the lid. Tea was always green, sweetened with a bit of sugar and, of course, love. Our kitchen table faced south, so they often sat across from each other in a flood of sunlight.

Tea in the summer meant pouring hot water over tea bags dropped into the taller pot—doubling the amount of tea used. Tall glasses were then filled to the top with ice cubes and a dash of sugar. After the tea steeped for a few minutes, it became iced tea—diluted to the proper strength because of the melting ice cubes. A sprig of mint from the ditch bank out back was sometimes picked ahead of time and placed in the top of each glass. If you've ever poured hot water over fresh mint, you know the smell is so compelling you can't help but stop whatever it is you're doing long enough to enjoy the bliss. If you haven't thought of it as bliss before, pay attention the next time someone takes a whiff of something heavenly like fresh mint. They always close their eyes, and for one tiny second, their faces take on that rapturous look that is unmistakably pure bliss.

Summer tea was always taken outside. Tea time for my parents was a regularly scheduled "meeting" to discuss the business of family and community.

Key to their ritual was the importance my mother assigned the vessels they used. Her pride and joy was her Jewel Tea dinnerware, collected one piece at a time. From the early 1900s up until the early '80s, Jewel Tea continued as a highly successful home delivery service, offering credit rewards. With every package of household products a customer bought, a credit was offered that could be applied toward payment for household articles without additional cash outlay. Much of the Autumn Leaf pattern pictured here entered American households in this manner. My mother's fifty-piece set is now a collector's item. Like a minister of holy things, my mother ritualized the care of her china. Food and the partaking of tea was her sacrament of love.

Butters backyard dining room, 1959

Since our house was so small, my mother moved us outside for our daily meals (right next to our cinderblock chicken coop), complete with an ironed tablecloth for every meal.

66

It [Jewel Tea china] is a cheerful combination that will promote good cheer at any meal. 99

– Needlecraft, The Home Arts Magazine, 1932

77

FOOD FOR A CAUSE

Planning an outdoor smorgasbord event requires plenty of table space for serving food. Since I wanted this event to be a moveable feast, I decided my collection of ironing boards was the perfect solution for flat, stable spaces here and there around my farm. Use this basic format and recipes to create your own backyard fundraiser that is destined to be an annual ritual no one will want to miss.

FAMILY OUTDOOR FESTIVAL

SATURDAY
AUG. 2
6:00 PM

You're Invited!

IRONING BOARD SMORGASBORD

COME AS YOU ARE. HARVEST AS YOU GO.
EAT AS YOU PLEASE!

SPECIAL ATTRACTIONS:

KIDS' PONY RIDES   ROLLING PIN THROWING CONTEST
FACE PAINTING   SPATULA RUN
MOON HOWL   KICK-THE-CAN

TAKE-HOME RECIPE CARDS FOR EVERYTHING SERVED!

FUNDRAISER TO BENEFIT:

PROJECT F.A.R.M.®
(FIRST-CLASS AMERICAN RURAL MADE)

ADMISSION $12
CHILDREN FREE!

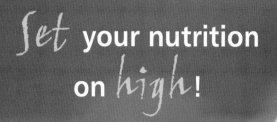

Set your nutrition
on _high_!

Eat
Your Veggies!

The best way to raise money for a cause is to sell food. I should know. I've organized probably fifty food events in my lifetime, raising sometimes thousands of dollars in one day. I think the more simple chili or spaghetti feeds are grand, but I prefer providing more than food and companionship. Think education. I like to send my guests home with a pocket full of recipes and inspiration for incorporating more veggies and homegrown or locally grown food in their daily diets. The next few pages of recipes do just that.

Eat your beets!

Momma Butters' Veggie Muffins (6 muffins)

For frustrated parents who find it hard to get their youngsters to eat vegetables, here's how my mother disguised them:

1   c vegetables
1   egg
2   c bread crumbs

Preheat oven to 350°F. Lightly oil muffin tins or use paper liners. Steam vegetables (use a single vegetable or any combination of vegetables) until soft. Mash with a potato masher. Stir in egg and bread crumbs. (My mother baked bread every week religiously her entire life, so if we hadn't eaten all her loaves when a new batch came out of the oven, she turned them into bread crumbs for meat loaves and veggie muffins.) Pour the mixture into your muffin tins and bake for 30–40 minutes. (My mother used different veggies to create color schemes for different holidays: spinach for St. Patrick's Day, carrots for Halloween, beets for Valentine's Day, etc.)

Eat your carrots!

Fewer than 15 percent
of grade-school-age children eat the recommended five or more daily servings of fruits and vegetables.

Eat your greens!

Doggedly
Deceptive
but Delicious!

Healthy Corn Doggies (6 muffins)

These are so good, your family won't care you're serving them the veggies you know they need to eat. And they hold up without crumbling—perfect for picnic baskets. Bring them to the ballpark and your kids won't ask for hot dogs.

1	c flour
1/3	c sugar
1	c cornmeal
2	t baking powder
3/4	t salt
1/3	c butter, cold, cut into 1/2-inch pieces
1	c vegetables, steamed and pureed (we used beets for one batch, carrots for another, and kale for the third)
1/2	c juice (or cooking liquid from vegetables)
1	egg, slightly beaten

Preheat oven to 425°F. Lightly oil a corn-shaped cornbread pan or muffin tin or use paper liners. Combine dry ingredients in a medium bowl. Cut in butter with a pastry blender. Combine vegetables, juice or cooking liquid, and egg. Stir into dry ingredients until just combined. Pour into pan or tin, filling 2/3 full. Bake for 25 minutes, until tops begin to brown.

Honey Mustard Spread

(approx. 3/4 cup)

1/2	c butter, softened
2	T dijon mustard,
2	T honey

In a small bowl, mix all ingredients until well combined.

A Root Crop
that
Measures Up

Momma Butters' Oven Fries

Here's a healthy twist on a side dish that everyone loves!

Potatoes
Olive oil
Salt

Preheat oven to 425°F. Wash potatoes, but don't peel. Cut into strips about 3/8-inch thick. Place potatoes in a bowl of ice water as you cut. Soak for 30 minutes. (This keeps the fries from soaking up too much oil when they cook.) Drain potatoes and pat dry with a dish towel. Return to bowl and toss with enough olive oil to coat. Bake in a single layer on a shallow pan until golden brown and tender, about 30–40 minutes. Sprinkle lightly with salt. Serve your oven fries with fry sauce (following page).

At this station, have some spading forks ready for a digging contest. Make wooden "measuring trays" ahead of time by cutting up old yardsticks into various sizes that are glued and nailed together for accommodating everything from "small fry" to "spud knocker" size potatoes. Have blue and red ribbons available for every imaginable size they might dig. Even the smallest potato "wins" a ribbon. For the older kids, have a game of *Farmopoly* handy. All properties, pieces, and cards are related to life on a farm. For 2–6 players, ages 8–adult, www.gamesbyjames.com.

Seasoned Oven Fries

Potatoes
Olive oil
1/2   c Parmesan cheese
2   T spice blend (pages 182–185)
Salt

In a large plastic bag, combine cheese and spice blend. Follow directions for Oven Fries (previous page). After coating with oil, add potatoes to bag, seal, and toss. Bake in a single layer on a shallow pan until golden brown and tender, about 30–40 minutes. Sprinkle lightly with salt. Serve your oven fries with fry sauce.

Healthier Fry Sauce

Mayonnaise
Ketchup

Mix equal parts mayonnaise and ketchup until well blended.

Note: When you get ready to make your fry sauce, look for ketchup and mayonnaise that doesn't have high-fructose corn syrup as an ingredient. Here's why. Until the 1970s, most sweetened processed foods used sugar made from sugar cane. But thanks to corporate chemists, that's been replaced with high-fructose corn syrup, which is made in a lab and cheaper to produce than sugar. It's in almost all sweet stuff like soda, ice cream, yogurt, cookies, candy, and juice. But it's also hiding in many brands of breads, cereals, crackers, canned fruit, salad dressings, ketchup, mayonnaise, and more.

Why should it be avoided? Because our bodies can't process it properly, nutrition experts blame high-fructose corn syrup for skyrocketing levels of diabetes and obesity in America. Plus, it can contribute to bone weakness and cancer. Paying a few cents more for sugar doesn't sound so bad, does it?

Avoiding high-fructose corn syrup isn't easy at first, but soon it becomes second nature. Start reading labels until you find items without it. Rule of thumb: The "organic" label is an easy assurance that you're not getting high-fructose corn syrup. For a list of high-fructose-free products, go to http://no-hfcs.tripod.com.

At this smorgasbord station, *everyone's a winner!*

Gum-wrapper Chains

Remember making gum-wrapper chains in the '50s? Fast forward to 2008, when Juicy Fruit meets Fifth Avenue. "Yummy" handbags made from 100 percent recycled candy wrappers once headed for the landfill are now a fashion statement … worth making. Ecoist (www.ecoist.com) works with Trees for the Future to plant a tree in areas affected by natural disasters and development for every bag sold. Offering accessories made from mostly repurposed and sustainable materials in fair trade, sweatshop-free environments, Ecoist hopes to inspire more people to think differently about the things they buy, how they are made, and where they come from.

'50s-Style Fun

Have you read the labels lately on what your children are eating at school and away from home? I quit chewing gum some thirty years ago, but recently for an office Halloween party, I decided the perfect addition to my costume would be a bowl of Juicy Fruit gum for sharing. But after a few memorable chews, something was different. Something was wrong. That's when I read the label. Juicy Fruit has joined the growing list of foods that are now sweetened artificially.

With the rapid rise in ADHD, autism, hyperactivity, and depression in children, parents need to start reading labels! Children are especially at risk for neurological disorders and should *not* be subjected to the chemicals found in artificially sweetened anything.

Momma Butters' Milk Punch Recipe

Combine 1 quart cold whole milk with 1/8 cup sugar (excellent with modern-day agave nectar as a substitute) and mix. Stir in one of the following combinations:

• 1/2 cup fresh lemon juice and 1/2 pint lemon sherbet
• 1 cup raspberry or strawberry jam and 1/2 pint vanilla ice cream
• 1 bottle ginger ale and 1/2 pint orange sherbet

On a mission to find gum without aspartame, I found it almost impossible to locate a mainstream gum that doesn't contain one or more chemical sugar substitutes. The best place to purchase gum is in a natural foods store. There, I found a brand made the way gum used to be made using cane sugar, glucose (about three-fourths as sweet as table sugar), and natural chicle. They even sell a "make your own gum kit" that lets you make your own healthy chewing gum right at home. Visit www.gleegum.com.

I hope that someday soon, pure complex raw sugars will be put back into gums, or better yet, healthy sweeteners like stevia and agave will find their way in. For now, make an effort to find safer alternatives. Chewing on sugar-free chemicals can result in headaches, mood swings, and even worse.

Momma Butters' Cakes 'n' Pies

"*Back then,* we were always outside and never hard up for something simple to keep us amused. "

May 20, 2007

Hi MaryJane! This is Susy from the old neighborhood in Ogden (Sue, Kris, Jeanne and Rea—your neighbors on Grant). Wow, I was reading a magazine, and imagine my surprise when the recipe I was reading made me decide to read the article and there you were! I was so excited that I called Kris and told her all about it; she can't wait to read it. We are so excited for you and all your success. You are our claim to fame! We know a celebrity! Hope you can e-mail back. I know you must be swamped. Just wanted to let you know how excited we are for you.

Susy

Susy, Susan, MaryJane, Jeanne, Judy, Kris, 1958

- -

June 5, 2007

How wonderful to hear from you!!! Tell me more. Where are you now? What are you doing? I spent close to six weeks alone in my parents' home when Momma died more than a year ago on Valentine's Day. I was sooooo happy to simply BE THERE and listen to the sounds I heard growing up, reminisce, crochet, sit. It was a huge comfort.

Hugs, MaryJane

- -

June 7, 2007

We heard about your mom too. You know she's happy to be with your dad. What great people they were and still are because they live on in our memories. I think of your mom often because she taught me how to knit. Remember the slippers we made Sandy when she was hit by a car when we were 10 and 11? And I think of camping, river floating, your mom's **Super Raspberry Shortcake**, and the rides in the back of the station wagon to J & K's for ice cream. And the homemade ice cream she made!

Keep safe. Susy

- -

June 14, 2007

This is so great to reconnect with you. I've been going through old family photos and I have the neatest picture of you and your sisters, Susan and Judy, holding rabbits in our backyard. Back then, we were always outside and never hard up for something simple to keep us amused. How are all of you? Are you all still in Ogden? I'll have to look you up when I am there next … a long overdue hug. We could reminisce to our hearts' content. I have many memories of you and your mother I'd like to share. Have you seen your old house lately? Sure do miss my mother …

Love, MaryJane

Momma Butters' Raspberry Shortcake
(4 large shortcakes)

2 2/3 c flour
1/3   c sugar
3 1/2 t baking powder
1   t salt
4   T butter, chilled
1 1/2 c half & half

Preheat oven to 425°F. Mix together dry ingredients in a large bowl. Cut in butter until it resembles coarse crumbs. Pour in half & half all at once, and beat for about 15 strokes with a wooden spoon until stiff dough forms. Do not overmix. Turn the dough out onto a lightly floured surface and knead gently about 8–10 times to smooth. Sprinkle with more flour if dough is too sticky. Shape dough into a log, divide into four equal parts, and shape into rough balls. Place on an ungreased baking sheet and bake for 18 minutes. Cool and top with fresh raspberries and real whipped cream.

Momma Butters' Rabbit Pot Pies (modernized) (8 servings)

Rabbit:

1	Rabbit, bone in
1	T thyme, chopped
1	T sage, chopped
1	t garlic, chopped
1/2	c madeira wine
1	t salt
1	t pepper
	Olive oil
1	qt stock

Sauce:

1/2	c mushrooms, dried, soaked, and chopped
1	medium onion, chopped
1	T garlic, chopped
1	t thyme and sage, dried, chopped
7	T butter, divided
1/2	c stock
1/2	c madeira wine
2	c cream
6	T flour

Filling:

2	c mushrooms
2	T shallots
1	T butter
2	c steamed root vegetables
2	c rabbit meat, chopped
2	sheets puff pastry

Rabbit: Combine all ingredients except stock and allow to marinate in covered baking dish for several hours. Add stock; braise rabbit at 400°F for one hour, until tender. Strain braising liquid and set aside. Pull meat from bone and chop. Set aside.

Preheat oven to 400°F.

Sauce: Sauté the first four ingredients in 1 T butter until soft. Add stock, wine, and cream and simmer until reduced by half. In a medium saucepan, make a roux: melt the remaining 6 T butter, stir in flour, and cook until light amber in color. Whisk into sauce. Adjust thickness, if necessary, with braising liquid. Continue to reduce until thick. Season with salt and pepper and set aside.

Filling: In a large pan, sauté the mushrooms and shallots in butter over medium heat. Remove from heat; add root vegetables (I used carrots, parsnips, potatoes, and beets) and cooked rabbit. Add two cups sauce. Mix well and keep warm. Divide filling among baking dishes and trim pastry to fit the top of each one (I used ten 3 1/2-inch antique gelatin molds). Bake for 15–20 minutes, or until golden brown.

*This recipe may also be made with chicken, omitting the braising step. Instead, cook chicken in the simmering stock on the stovetop until thoroughly cooked and tender.

> " There is nothing better on a cold wintry day than a properly made pot pie. "
>
> – Craig Claiborne

This is my younger brother Rex standing in front of one of our rabbit pens. In addition to raising our own rabbits and chickens for meat, we filled our freezer with venison and fish. It was my parents' way of making sure we ate only the best.

Rabbit Pot Pies

Sauce:
½ cup dried mushrooms, soaked and chop
1 medium onion, chopped
1 T garlic, chopped
2 t each thyme and sage, dried or fresh le
½ cup chicken stock
2 cups cream

Saute first three ingredients in 2 T butter for 10
minutes. Add remaining ingredients and simmer until
reduced by half.

Bug-out on Work!

Momma Butters' Bug Repellant for Plants (1 gallon)

4   large onions
12   cloves garlic

Boil for 45 minutes in 1 gallon water. Cool and strain. Spray on infected plants.

When you're trying to teach your children to harvest a crop diligently, set up a "relief station" that speaks playful and fun. For strawberries, set out a bowl of sour cream and a bowl of brown sugar—your kids will have a messy good time! And since you and your plants need occasional relief from pesky bugs, set up a station to guarantee they'll bug off quickly!

" Green blades of grass and warbling birds, children that gambol and play, the clouds of heaven above. "

– Walt Whitman

Bug-off Bars (12 small bars)

3   oz beeswax

1 1/2 c cocoa butter

2   oz sweet almond oil

3   drops vitamin E

10   drops bug repellant essential oils
      (Cedarwood, citronella, eucalyptus, geranium, lemongrass,
      and sandalwood are known to help repel insects. For our
      bug bars, we chose cedarwood, citronella, and eucalyptus
      as fragrances that melded well.)

Melt beeswax, cocoa butter, and almond oil in the top of a double
boiler. Remove from heat and stir in vitamin E and the essential
oils. Pour contents into a child's muffin tin and let the bars cool
completely. Rub bar over skin. Not only does it repel insects, it has
ingredients to nourish skin and make it silky soft!

Cracker Jill (approx. 17 cups)

1/2   c popcorn kernels, freshly popped
3/4   c butter
3/4   c sugar
3   T coffee
2   T maple syrup
1/4   t salt
1   c peanuts

Bring butter, sugar, coffee, and syrup to a boil in a medium saucepan. Reduce heat and simmer for 5 minutes. Add salt and peanuts to popcorn; coat with butter mixture.

You know those fabulous potato chips that come in a million different flavors, but cost a fortune? Here's my healthier (and cheaper) alternative. For optimum health, use an air popper.

Honey Dijon Popcorn

(approx. 17 cups)
1/2   c popcorn kernels, freshly popped
3   T butter
1/4   c honey
2   T + 2 t dijon mustard

Heat butter, honey, and mustard until melted in a medium saucepan. Toss with popcorn.

Popcorn

Trail Mix Popcorn
(approx. 20 balls)

1/2	c popcorn kernels, freshly popped
1/2	c pumpkin seeds,
1	c dried banana chips
3/4	c craisins
1/4	c barley malt
1/4	c brown rice syrup
1	t vanilla

Toss popcorn with pumpkin seeds, bananas, and craisins. Heat barley malt and syrup in a medium saucepan; add vanilla. Pour over popcorn mixture; toss well. Form into balls.

Find a crochet pattern for this unique hotpad on my website, www.maryjanesfarm.org/categories/stitching-room.asp.

Chocolate Lovers' Popcorn
(approx. 9 cups)

1/4	c popcorn kernels, freshly popped
1/2	c sugar
1/2	c agave syrup
1/4	c butter
1/2	t salt
2	T cocoa

Bring sugar, syrup, butter, salt, and cocoa to a boil in a medium saucepan. Toss with popcorn.

Herbed Popcorn
(approx. 17 cups)

1/2	c popcorn kernels, freshly popped
5	T butter, melted
2	t basil, dried
2	t oregano, dried
2	t onion powder
2	t granulated garlic
1/2	t salt

Toss popcorn with remaining ingredients.

Cheesy Popcorn
(approx. 17 cups)

1/2	c popcorn kernels, freshly popped
5	T butter, melted
1/2	t salt
1/3	c cheese powder

Toss popcorn with butter and salt; coat with cheese powder.

Cheesy Barbeque Popcorn
(approx. 17 cups)

1/2	c popcorn kernels, freshly popped
1/4	c butter
2	T olive oil
1	t garlic powder
1/2	t onion powder
1	t chili powder
1/2	t salt
1/2	t Wrights hickory flavoring
1/2	c Parmesan cheese, finely grated

Melt butter in a medium saucepan; add olive oil and spices. Toss with popcorn; sprinkle with cheese.

Salt & Pepper Popcorn
(approx. 17 cups)

1/2	c popcorn kernels, freshly popped
1/3	c olive oil
1/2	t salt
1	t pepper, freshly ground
1	t garlic powder

Toss popcorn with remaining ingredients.

Cinnamon Popcorn
(approx. 17 cups)

1/2	c popcorn kernels, freshly popped
1	c pecans, chopped
1/2	c brown rice syrup
1/4	c maple syrup
2	t cinnamon
1/8	t salt

Combine popcorn and pecans in a large bowl. Heat syrups in a medium saucepan; add cinnamon and salt. Toss with popcorn.

Peanut Butter & Jelly Popcorn
(approx. 17 cups)

1/2	c popcorn kernels, freshly popped
1/4	c agave syrup
1/2	c peanut butter
1/2	c raspberry jam
1	t vanilla

Heat sweetener, peanut butter, and jam until melted in a medium saucepan; add vanilla. Toss with popcorn.

Hollowed-out gourds and baby squash make lovely gift vases for your guests as they leave. You can fill them with water and add fresh flowers along with some dried grasses. My favorite flowers for gourd vases are old-fashioned zinnias. They have a strong stem, they last for weeks, and they come in every color of the rainbow. If you grow only one outdoor flower, let it be zinnias!

Welcome to Our Farmhouse
LIFE IS GOOD

Fresh Air
Stargazing
Love and Romance
Quiet Spaces
Honest Folks

OUTRIGGED

Picnics & Weekend CAMPING

When it comes time to put your beloved work truck "out to pasture" because she's no longer road worthy, keep in mind she's still capable of the occasional moonlighting job—giving new meaning to the term "truck bed."

" Thousands of tired, nerve-shaken, overcivilized people are beginning to find out that going to the mountains is going home; that *wilderness is a necessity.* "

– John Muir

IN THIS CHAPTER

THE Art OF THE PICNIC

Family Picnic Kit (right)

Think of a picnic kit the same way you would a first-aid kit. In other words, be prepared! But in this case, the unexpected is what you're hoping for. The next time everyone's a tad cranky and tired of the same old routine or you're thinking about another restaurant meal, grab your family picnic kit, prepacked with the bare essentials (I like vintage linens and enamelware), and head out. Make a quick stop for some fixins and fruit. You're good to go in minutes.

In this section, you'll dig out your old suitcases and hatboxes and turn them into ready-to-go picnic baskets full of the accessories you'll need to complement the food and set the mood for a perfect picnic.

The Perfect Place for a Picnic

Picking the perfect site to set up a cozy meal takes just a bit of planning. Since a wild-goose chase to find that perfect place can leave you pulling your hair out, it's a good idea to either go to a place you know well or scope out a special spot beforehand. In general, look for shady locations with easy vehicle access and plenty of privacy. You don't want to hike far with all your food and put a damper on the festive mood.

Consider what sort of setting you enjoy. If you like a tidy, mowed environment with shady trees and public restrooms, a nice city park with lots of green space is ideal. But if you're feeling more intrepid, a secluded spot in a National Forest or other natural recreation area makes for a refreshingly "out there" adventure.

A unique off-the-beaten-path destination with historical charm and mystery is the rural cemetery. In the early 1800s, while industrialization was picking up speed, the romantic aesthetic of rural innocence still beckoned. Residents of the burgeoning cities were losing their connection with nature, and many feared that crowding would lead to moral decline within society. Before the development of public parks, the "rural cemetery movement" sought to make nature accessible to the urban population. Large tracts of land were landscaped not only for the dead but also for the living, and the park-like settings that resulted were civic institutions designed for public use. People could gather and enjoy the pastoral environment they felt was essential to their well-being. The rural cemetery became a destination for rejuvenation and social recreation. Families picnicked on the plots purchased for their eventual resting grounds as horse-drawn carriages followed meandering roadways throughout hillsides, lakes, and lawns planted to mimic wilder settings. Today, many of these historic cemeteries are designated landmarks and are lovely, intriguing places to visit.

If you want to picnic close to home, though, get creative. You can transform a garden, rooftop, treehouse, or back porch into an outpost retreat!

Car Camping

Car camping, unlike backpacking, gets you right to your campsite without having to lug all your gear on your back. It's a perfect way to get in touch with nature without a bunch of hard work. And there are countless beautiful, easy-access outdoor destinations from beaches to the backwoods.

When you're "gypsying," as car camping was called in the 1900s, you pack your car with gear and drive to a countryside camp where you can relax in the open air with many of the comforts of home. Sleep in a cabin, a tent, or build a lean-to with tree branches and canvas. Catch fish and cook them over a campfire. It's just rugged enough to feel adventurous.

Butters Family Gypsy Camp, 1950s

Discover nearly 300 places to picnic nationwide, plus photos, maps and more at "Where to Picnic in America," www.alanskitchen.com/PICNICKING .

Kent, MaryJane, and Scott, weekend camping, 1958

"We simply need to know that wild country is available to us, even if we never do more than drive to its edge and look in. For it can be a means of reassuring ourselves of our sanity."

– Wallace Stegner

Game Picnic Kit (left)

When it comes to car camping, you need to have a game plan ... prepacked and ready to go. Our childhood favorites were Scrabble and Yahtzee. Search out some of the tried-and-true classics like Cribbage or Dominoes. Don't forget to toss in a deck of cards.

My son made this lightweight mini-barbeque out of an empty five-gallon can. He used a riveter to attach the handles and legs made from juice cans. Teach your kids the three R's: reuse, remake, revive! Think salvage whenever you can.

THE PERFECT PICNIC FARE

Since potato salads are a staple at most any picnic and barbecuing is a favorite summer pastime, here's a great way to combine the two: *roasted* potato salads. Perfect for picnics or on the grill at home, other foods like sandwiches and chicken tag along easily.

The first step is baking the potatoes ahead of time. A few of our favorites that we grow here on the farm are Red Desiree and Yukon Gold, but any ole tater will do. Bake the potatoes as you normally would, but remove them from the oven the minute they are done. Over-baking will make them difficult to skewer. You want them slightly al dente. Allow the potatoes to cool completely before making the recipe. Cut the potatoes, skins and all, into 3/4-inch cubes and then skewer them. Brush the potatoes generously with olive oil, and sprinkle with salt and pepper. Place skewers on a grill top and cook, turning frequently, until golden brown and crispy. Remove from the grill and toss with other ingredients while still warm. (See ingredient suggestions on the following pages.)

Smoked Bacon and Mustard Salad

Smoked Bacon and Mustard Salad

(6 servings)
6   c grilled potatoes (page 107)
3   small shallots
3   T olive oil
3   T whole-grain mustard
2   T red wine vinegar
1/2 t salt
Pepper, freshly cracked
3   slices smoked bacon,
     cooked and crumbled
3   T parsley, fresh, chopped

Sauté shallots in olive oil until
barely softened, remove from
heat and add mustard, vinegar,
salt, pepper. Toss with warm
potatoes, bacon, and parsley.
Serve immediately.

Fennel and Chimichurri Salad

(6 servings)
6   c grilled potatoes (page 107)
1   bulb fennel, thinly sliced
1/3 c Chimichurri Sauce
(Chimichurri is a slightly spicy South
American condiment made of oil,
vinegar, and fresh herbs.)

Mix all ingredients for
Chimichurri Sauce and let stand
at room temperature for 2
hours. Toss with warm potatoes
and fennel. Serve immediately.

Chimichurri Sauce (1 1/2 cups)
1/4 c onion, finely chopped
1/2 c parsley, finely chopped
3   T cilantro, finely chopped
3   cloves garlic, minced
1/2 t salt
1/2 t cumin, ground
1/2 t red pepper, crushed
1/4 t black pepper, ground
1/2 c olive oil
1/4 c red wine vinegar

Southwestern Salad

(6 servings)
6   c grilled potatoes (page 107)
1   c fresh corn, cooked
1   roasted red pepper, chopped
1/4 c red onion, finely chopped
2   cloves garlic, minced
2   T cilantro, finely chopped
2   T olive oil
2   T red wine vinegar
1/2 t salt
Pepper, freshly cracked

Toss all ingredients with warm
potatoes. Serve immediately.

Southwestern Salad

Fennel and Chimichurri Salad

Friendship Picnic Kit (left)

A good way to show a girlfriend how much you cherish her friendship is to surprise her with a picnic planned just for her. Don't worry too much about a well-rounded meal. This type of excursion calls for chocolate, cheese, crackers and tea!

The Girlfriends Game

The perfect accessory for your next girls' picnic is "the one and only game about women for women" (www.cowgirlsgame.com). Celebrate your life, dreams, hopes, loves, passions, secrets, and challenges while you swap tales and explore self.

You'll answer questions like:
- What led to your first kiss?
- If you woke up in the morning and you found yourself as a man, what are the first three things you would do?
- What is the one thing you would buy yourself if money were no object?

M**Y FRIENDSHIPS WITH**

WOMEN GIVE ME A DEEPER

EXPERIENCE OF MYSELF.

AMY LAWRENCE 1889

Vintage Hat Box Emergency Road Kit

- Candle
- Chocolate
- Duct Tape
- Emergency Phone Numbers
- First Aid Kit
- Flares
- Flashlight (and extra batteries)
- Jumper Cables
- Matches (in waterproof container)
- Pocket Knife
- Rope or Bungee Cord
- Sewing Kit
- Small Bills and Change
- Space Blanket
- Water
- Whistle

> After a big account told me, *'Hey, girlie,* I don't do business with women,' I started wearing hats with big brims. It was self-defense. I needed some armor to wear into battle every day. After 28 years in the business, I have a collection of 45 hats. It's my signature.

– Lenore Janis, President of Professional Women in Construction

Office Picnic Kit (right)

For your next office birthday party, why not pull a picnic out of your hat … box? Gussy up that treasured vintage hatbox tucked away in the back of your closet. Make it extra special by using pretty serving trays and vintage rhinestone-embellished hanky napkins. On your way to work, simply pick up some yummy organic cheese, crackers and an apple or two!

LOOKING BACK …

When I read Lenore Janis' quote about hats (left) in *Working Woman*, I recalled the following scene. Back in the '70s, I was at the end of my second season working for the U.S. Forest Service as a Wilderness Ranger. At this time, I was one of three females ever hired for this kind of job. Another employee, maybe thirty years older than me and married, tried to pick me up in a bar one night when I was shooting pool with the locals. I let him know I wasn't the least bit interested. Our next meeting was less cordial. I had just finished a ten-day hitch in the wilderness when I was called by radio to come into the head ranger's office. There sat my "spurned lover" in the ranger's seat. When my boss accepted a transfer, he had been appointed temporary acting ranger. He told me to pack my bags. My season was over and someone else would patrol my area.

I was wearing a big cowboy hat that day. My eyes instantly welled up. I pleaded with him, but he leaned close and said, "I'm just separating the men from the boys."

The John Wayne hat I wore that day had always made my step a bit bolder. I remember to this day how I felt in that hat when, eyes dry, I left his office … striding. I contacted a lawyer to file a discrimination lawsuit. After he sent a couple of letters to the Forest Service and I received a bill for his services that equaled a month's pay, I knew I needed to move on and put it behind me. A short time later, I landed my dream job as a Wilderness Station Guard.

Some twenty years later, an old friend called to tell me her husband was going through training for a Wilderness Ranger position in the same district where I was "laid off." They now hired fifteen rangers instead of two. As part of their two-day training, their leader (the district mechanic when I worked there) described the work and attitude of the "best ranger we've ever had." My friend's husband went up after and asked if he was talking about me. Yup, he was, and I was finally vindicated. He said he had often thought about me and felt bad about what happened. As he wondered aloud where I ended up, he added, "Please tell her if she ever wants her job back, it's hers."

HARVEST DAY PICNICS

In the corner of my soon-to-be commercial farm kitchen, I've created a little "nook of nostalgia." Amidst my more modern-day furnishings—high-pressure canners, industrial-grade mixers, and more—I've pulled three generations of my husband's family back into our lives using the gentle reminder of his mother's "Home Comfort" range dressed up in the type of graniteware once used for their harvest-day picnics and threshing parties. My "past-to-present" project involved retrieving her rusty range from the back of our barn and addressing about thirty years worth of neglect. After applying some elbow grease, it was ready to tell its story again.

My husband Nick's grandfather, a farmer in Kansas, moved his family to Montana to farm, hoping to avoid hearing the sound of his neighbor's axe—his definition of overpopulation. After going broke there, they moved back to Kansas. The second time he had the urge to leave Kansas, he held an auction and sold absolutely everything. "He even sold the dog that was my best friend," said my father-in-law Ivan, age ninety-seven.

Nick's grandfather then bought a Model T, and the family (two adults and three children) drove south to Arizona. Driving through the desert was difficult, but the state had laid down miles and miles of planks to drive on. They also kept a constant patrol of men on horseback in case anyone's car stalled. It was so hot, you'd die quickly if you couldn't get help. Nick's grandparents decided Arizona was too hot

once they got there, so they wandered on over to the coast, traveling up and then inland. They ended up buying land outside of Moscow, Idaho, the farm my husband will inherit someday.

At the time they bought their farm, they also bought eighty acres a hundred miles south of here that Ivan eventually inherited and later sold for only $10,000. When Nick's father and mother, Ivan and Ruth, needed to work that ground or harvest its wheat, they lived in a tent onsite. Ivan would work the fields in the mornings while Ruth cooked food for everyone on a wood stove. During lunch, Ivan and Ruth would switch and she'd go work the fields while everyone else ate. Ivan remembers fondly, "Ruth was great in the kitchen, but she could easily do the work of a man."

"Don't Throw It Away" the ad reads, "Mend It With Mendets" instead! Perfect for mending the boilers Ivan and Ruth used for heating water or the enamelware they used for cooking, the back of the package also said, "Indispensible for Campers." My modern-day take on the concept lets me turn leaky pots and pans into things like planters or bathing dippers. The bread saver pot on the left is now a vessel for the bird food I dispense daily. To fix a hole, put something like a round piece of an old rubber work glove with a hole punched in the middle or a rubber plumbing washer against one side with a metal washer placed on top. Push the screw through, then attach a second metal washer on the opposite side. Put a nut on the screw and tighten. The rubber will seal the hole.

1950s mend... still holding tight!

For me, birdsong is the happiest, most carefree sound on earth. That unexpected moment of winged merriment and playful pause can stop me in my tracks, completely redirecting my thoughts. And some birds are so colorful they're like little fireworks shooting off—a visual "tweet" treat as well. But I'm always left wanting more. For that reason, and because songbird habitat is increasingly in peril, I've found I can easily meet their need for a safe home using junk that I scrounge, the ultimate in re-use and make-do. When you find enamelware so old it is "beyond" Mendets, incorporate them into your birdhouses as shown here. Even if you don't have a big backyard, or a yard at all, you can join in by putting a birdhouse on your balcony. If your home doesn't have a balcony, try a windowsill, extended by a board. To put out more food, just raise the window.

Streamlining
YOUR LIFE

AIRSTREAM | LAND YACHT | Safari

Nothing streamlines your life like a reduction in the square footage of your living space. An Airstream trailer is the best of all worlds ... it's a small home, it's the open-road, it's the wind in your hair, it's life off the beaten path.

> " Tell me, what is it you plan to do with your one wild and precious life. "
> – Mary Oliver

Land Yacht

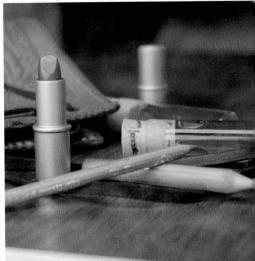

T R A M P I N G
Taking It On the Road

Pregnant with my first child and intentionally homeless except for the 14-foot travel trailer shown here peeking out from behind where I posed for a photograph with my best friend Sara, I spent months four and five of my pregnancy on the road behind the wheel of my '53 pickup truck, pulling a two-toned pink and yellow-trimmed "grown-up dollhouse." Those two months were to be the last of my tramping (trailer camping) days—I've been rooted ever since. In fact, by the time Meg was born, I'd just moved onto a ranch and into a house in White Bird, Idaho. An unexpected

"Orville," my FORD (Fix Or Repair Daily) 1953 pickup truck complete with trailer hitch.

Actress Joyce Holden is crowned "Miss Trailer Life" in preparation for the opening of the 1955 Trailer Life Show.

. . . .

How about a tiny house that you can pull behind you on the road or perch permanently? For unique eco-friendly tiny houses, check out www.tumbleweedhouses.com .

> 66 When the *whole world is your living room,* a tiny house seems plenty. 99
>
> – Jay Shafer
> Tumbleweed Tiny House Company

. . . .

C-section put me in debt $900, the exact amount I got when I sold my trailer. I'll bet you can't get a C-section today for $900, or likewise a vintage trailer in mint condition.

"Wildflower" was a beauty, inside and out. Her previous owners were my parents, so she was a familiar companion to me. But like a child put up for adoption, I've often wondered if I'll bump into her again somewhere, somehow.

Her interior was a study in the utilization of space. Everything had its designated place. Her charming interior was mostly wood with pine veneer cabinets and very little plastic, although music in that era was still plenty vinyl, the likes of which John Prine sang "Pink Cadillac" and Nanci Griffith sang "Montana Backroads" to me whenever I could find a plug-in for my portable record player.

My mother had kept Wildflower clean as a whistle, and I learned how to make her floors and counters shine. When she wasn't on the road for family outings in the late '60s, she became an oversized "playhouse" for me and my gaggle of girlfriends.

I've never gotten over my love of small spaces, where everything has its place and every square inch serves a purpose. When I'm out and about and I see a trailer coming, I wonder if maybe this time, it'll be her! I do miss her gleaming skin, her hand-crank windows, her ovoid profile, and her unapologetic Spartan style. Trailer for sale or rent . . . Queen of the Road!

Deanna Keahey, "Adventurous Wench," designs trips just for women who can't resist the urge to travel to the far corners of the earth and back. www.adventurouswench.com

With a pair of tin snips and leather gloves, common tin cans can be "born again" as decorative candle holders.

What are we talking about here? The women who "tramp" or the trailers they inhabit? Since both require an enticing exterior as well as an inviting interior, their distinctive types are interchangeable. For the most part, vintage trailer designs fall into three groups:

Bread Loaf: Her "fresh-from-the-oven" slightly rounded corners and roof edges seem to best suit the type who desires to have a trailer serve as a permanent home if need be. Many of the late 1930s and early '40s "build-your-own" designs fell into this category. They were rectangular and practical, never too curvaceous. With flat sides and only slightly bowed roof lines, her interior was conventional and her thinking "inside the box." The bread loaf type is the one that grew and grew into the manufactured homes we see today.

Canned Ham: As practical and safe as a boxed-in life may be, it isn't as exciting to look at as the aerodynamically and curvaceous "canned ham" type. Somewhat ovoid (egg-shaped, a smaller

"point" on one end than the other), the canned ham became popular when the idea of "streamlining your life" finally hit the trailer industry. Manufacturers went for the canned ham shape and she became all the rage by the time the '50s rolled around. Often sporting two-toned paint jobs, canned hams were more about roadworthiness than size. Compact enough to actually take on the road, they make good travel companions.

Teardrop: Keeping an eye on exciting new curves, the canned ham trailer morphed into the teardrop. Easily towed behind any car, the teardrop turned weekend trailer camping into romantic getaways. Her tiny interior slept two people and her kitchen was accessed from an outer rear hatch. With names like "Runlite" and "Wild Goose," she is the ultimate tramper's camper.

OUTSPOKEN...

Every summer, **Lois Blackburn**, age seventy-five, packs her viola and succumbs to the gypsy blood that calls her back to the road. There's an annual trip to New Mexico to see her children, of course. But there are also excursions into Idaho's nooks and crannies. She fuels up the mini-motorhome she calls her gypsy wagon and puts in a supply of food for herself and a big sack of dog food for her faithful companion, Lulu.

She stops at small-town cafes, laundromats, grocery stores. "I like to talk to the people," she says. And she watches for signs. "They may say something like 'come see our museum.' That's how I found the museum at St. Gertrude's Monastery in Cottonwood. That's how I've discovered three of Idaho's historical ranger stations."

The Tin Can Tourists, founded in 1919, was an organization whose members sported a tin can mounted on the radiator cap of their "Tin Lizzies." Their stated goals included "high moral values, and clean and wholesome entertainment." They held regular campouts and elected a leader known as the "Mayor of Easy Street." By 1938, the organization had grown to 30,000 members, and 100,000 members by 1963. Some ninety years after their inception, TCTer's are still hanging out the welcome sign (www.tincantourists.com).

In my own hometown every July, five hundred RV enthusiasts meet at the University of Idaho campus in Moscow for a week of classes and activities focusing on the practical how-to's of fulltime RV'ing. The "Life on Wheels" conference (www.lifeonwheels.com) offers an amazing buffet of information, classes, networking, and even before and after caravans. Throughout the five days, about two hundred courses are offered on topics as diverse as cooking, destinations, photography, self-defense, and exercise.

Lois, who retired at age sixty-seven from her university job teaching music education, says, "I'm very blessed to have a life like this. I plan to stretch it out as far as I can. Now when everybody else is going back to school, I'm still out camping."

Any summer day, in a deep-woods Idaho campground, you might see a gypsy wagon, a black and tan dog, and Lois, her silver-blond head bent over a viola, sending sweet strains of music out onto pine-pungent air.

Glamping
THE ROMANCE OF THE ROAD

Glamping (glamour camping) has finally come into its own. It's the juxtaposition of rugged and really pretty, grit and glam, diesel and absolutely darling! My pink diesel rig (painted by my son to match my favorite color of fingernail polish) actually runs on homegrown biofuel. A glam gal really can have it all these days!

Glamping is ...
ALL GIRL, ALL GLAM, ALL GROWN UP!

"It's way better than a
Barbie doll camping set!
Bigger!"

— Juli Thorson

"Reel" Women

You get a line, I'll get a pole ...

If you've ever had the urge to go fishing, now's the time. Women are wading into the water in droves, breaking free of the fisherman stereotype and referring to ourselves simply as "fishers." The beauty of this stampede is that we're finding sustenance that goes far beyond the flesh of the fish we catch. The dynamics of fishing connect us intimately with the natural world. Gentle, deliberate movements in repetitive meter are punctuated by patient silences, creating a sense of meditative calm that soothes the soul.

"Yes, it's about the line and these wild flashes of light you see in the stream, but it's really the water that we go to and the water we've always gone to. For some kind of solace, for understanding, for cleansing, for rebirth," flyfisher Margot Page explains in *Fly-Fishing for Sharks: An American Journey*, by Richard Louv.

Indeed, water shimmers, flows, and cycles. It moves with a grace that is undeniably feminine, and when we dip into it, we feel at home. With more than 17 million licensed female anglers in the U.S., it's clear that women are reclaiming their right to America's last sacred sport ... with a passion. If you're unfamiliar with the territory, you'll find lots of helping hands to guide you on your journey—from bait, flies, and old-timer tricks to fillets in the frying pan, we are learning from one another.

So, come on, let's head down to the fishin' hole ...

LET IT LURE YOU
Guides, Outfitters, and Workshops for Reel Women

• **Casting for Recovery:** Fly fishing retreats for women affected by breast cancer. www.castingforrecovery.org
• **Reel Women Fly Fishing Adventures:** Fishing trips, fishing schools, and guide schools for women. www.reel-women.com
• **Women Anglers Online:** Online fishing magazine for female anglers. www.womenanglers.us
• **The Women's Wilderness Institute:** Women-specific courses in fly fishing and other outdoor activities. www.womenswilderness.org
• **Ladies, Let's Go Fishing!** Training and hands-on seminars teaching fishing techniques. www.ladiesletsgofishing.com
• **International Women's Fishing Association:** Angling competitions for women. www.iwfa.org

Check with your local Fish and Game office for women-only outdoor programs close to home.

Take me fishing.
So we can catch a fish THIS big.

Take me fishing.
And teach me the things grandma taught you.

Take me fishing.
And I'll remember it forever.

takemefishing.org

You'll find boating and fishing information—everything from how to bait a hook, to trailering a boat, to tips for fishing with kids, to recipes and more—at this website created by the nonprofit Recreational Boating and Fishing Foundation.

reel little women

THE
Bait
DEBATE

" *Luck* affects everything; let your hook always be cast. In the stream where you least expect it, there will be a fish. "

– Ovid

The debate between proponents of fly fishing and advocates of the "bait and wait" method has raged for decades. There are fishers staunchly devoted to either camp, each believing their method to be superior. The truth is that both have been used for eons, and both can be very effective means of catching fish. So, what's all the fuss about?

First of all, fly fishing has a certain snob appeal. It requires grace and rhythm, and a perfect cast appears elegant and artful in its execution. It also takes patience, stealth, and at least a vague grasp of entomology, since a flyfisher must choose her flies according to the latest insect hatch. But, there is a degree of skill involved in operating a sinker rig as well. The bait fisher studies the water to determine the best location for her hook, and she becomes deft at casting right to the spot in spite of branches, boulders, and other obstacles in her path.

So, could it be the financial investment that generates sparks between the parties? A bait fisher can boast catching fish on a $30 setup, whereas a flyfisher may flaunt fish hooked on hundreds of dollars' worth of high-end equipment. Or maybe it's just whether or not you're willing to touch a worm.

The reason for the rift may never be clear, but there's one thing both sides agree on: the most important aspect of fishing is getting outdoors and extending hook, line, and hope into the water.

" *All you need* to be a fisher[wo]man is patience and a worm. "

– Herb Shriner

PAYING IT FORWARD 101

You likely remember your very first fishing trip and who took you. Odds are pretty good that positive first-time experience is why you're still fishing today. That's what an organization called Anglers' Legacy is all about: giving back what you've been given. A group of folks from across the country are pledging to pay it forward. They're taking family members, co-workers, neighbors, acquaintances, even the mechanics who work on their cars fishing for the first time. Take the pledge! www.anglerslegacy.org

And whether you're interested in trying fly fishing for the first time or you're a professional in the field, the International Women Fly Fishers wants to support you and connect you with other women with the same interest: fly fishing. In addition to information about the organization itself, their website provides a growing and dynamic library of information about fly fishing and women fly fishing professionals. www.intlwomenflyfishers.org

Hooked
ON '50s-STYLE FISHING
a stick ...   a string ... a hook

In 1953, the year I was born:

Little Ricky was born on the TV show, *I Love Lucy*.

A new car cost $1,650, a new house $9,500, and the average annual income was $4,000.

Gasoline was 20 cents per gallon.

New York adopted the three-color traffic light.

Fabric was 17 cents a yard.

Jacqueline Auriol became the second woman flier to break the sound barrier.

Walt Disney's *Peter Pan* premiered.

1953		**MAY**			1953	
5TH MONTH					31 DAYS	
SUN	MON	TUE	WED	THU	FRI	SAT
	6th LAST Q.	13th NEW M.	20th FIRST Q.	28th FULL M.	1	2
3	4	5	6	7	8	9
10	11	12	13	14	15	16
17	18	19	20	21	22	23
24/31	25	26	27	28	29	30

I can't think of a single word I heard more as a kid from my parents than "GREAT"! I used it with equal frequency on my own kids. Even now, I struggle to find its replacement when I write: here's a great way to … this makes a great gift …

But when it comes to kids, you can't say the word too much. The look on a child's face when told they're GREAT or they've done something great is a public service announcement of sorts because that great kid can't help but grow up to be great—great at something or great at many things. It's a great thing, a kid that's great!

Every kid on earth loves nothing more that proving their greatness, whether it's done with a hammer, a pad of paper and pencil, a ball, or their own two legs pumping higher and higher on a swing. How many times did I hear, "Mom, watch!"?

Nothing evokes greatness more than fishing. Think of its components. If you were to design a greatness boot camp, you'd need to come up with something that involves patience and diligence, then thrilling, and finally—great!

As a youngster, I was a fishing fanatic, thanks to my parents. And somewhere along the "line," I was told I was great at cleaning fish too—a great way to sucker me into cleaning everyone's fish. I took great pride (that great word again) in how cold my hands got, how thoroughly I cleaned along the spine, how fast I worked. But the component of fishing that I think was of most value to me was the catch the night before, the worms. My brothers and I turned it into a lucrative little business selling to local shops and greeting customers in our own backyard. I learned about commerce and customer service, marketing. At some point, a famous TV personality, Fireman Frank (a local rendition of Captain Kangaroo), discovered us and proclaimed to the world, "Those Butters kids have the best night crawlers in Utah!" For 25 cents a dozen, we headed to our lawn every night with flashlights and fast fingers to catch what would eventually catch a fish. So yeah, I'm forever hooked on fishing with worms. It's just a great way to catch fish!

Tip: For more on fishing with kids, see my first book, *MaryJane's Ideabook, Cookbook, Lifebook—For the Farmgirl in All of Us*.

MaryJane, 1957

I like to fish with bait … not elegant, like fly fishing, but it usually gets some fish into the frying pan.

– Juli Thorson

MaryJane, 1964

Fishing with Kids

Fishing is a fun way to introduce kids to nature while teaching them the values of stewardship and "living off the land." But your chances of instilling a lifelong love of the sport are far better when the fish are biting, so be prepared to fish when it's hot and leave when it's not. Here are a few other kid-tested secrets of success:

★ Pick a place that is easy access, comfortable, and safe.

★ Provide your youngster with simple small-sized tackle in good working order.

★ Use live bait to increase the chance of catching fish. (Besides, worms, minnows, and crawdads are fascinating all by themselves!)

★ Start out by casting and hooking fish yourself, then let your child reel them in. As her confidence grows, you can teach her how to cast, notice nibbles, and set a hook.

★ Bring snacks, sunscreen, insect repellent, and first-aid basics.

★ Have patience, lots of it. You'll have to bait hooks, unsnag lines, and release fish while your child splashes, falls down, and rolls in the sand.

★ Keep it fun by focusing on your child's efforts as well as her catch record.

Tackle Box
Check List
✓ Hooks, sinkers, bobbers, lures, flies
✓ Bait
✓ Fishing pliers for removing hooks
✓ Line clippers
✓ Camera to record your catch
✓ Insect repellent
✓ Sunscreen
✓ Water and snacks
✓ Small first aid kit and hand sanitizer

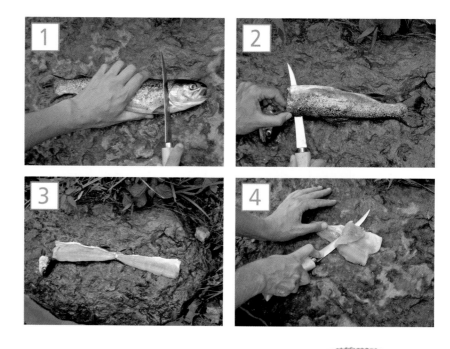

How to Fillet a Fish

1. After you've gutted the fish, lay it on its side on a cutting board (or a good, flat rock if you're in the outpost), and keep it as cool as possible during the fileting process. Using a sharp fillet knife, make the first cut behind the gills, as if you're going to cut off the head. Cut only until the knife touches the backbone (don't cut the head off completely).

2. Insert the knife near the spine and cut gently down the length of the fish from gills to tail, barely touching the ribcage with the under side of your blade while using the backbone as a guide, so that the meat "peels" away from the bones.

3. Continue cutting until you cut the fillet off at the tail. Flip the fish over and repeat on the other side.

4. With each fillet laying skin side down, remove the skin by inserting the knife at the tail end and slicing the meat from the skin.

Tip: My father grew better roses than anyone. He claims it was because he buried fish remains around his bushes (fish fertilizer)!

Herb-Crusted Trout with Garlic Spinach

(4 servings)

8	boneless and skinless trout fillets, seasoned with salt and pepper
2	T dijon mustard
3/4	c bread crumbs
1	t chopped fresh tarragon
1	t chopped fresh thyme
1	t chopped fresh parsley
1	t chopped fresh chives
2	t butter
1	T olive oil
2	garlic cloves, peeled and finely chopped
4	c fresh baby spinach

Salt and pepper to taste

Coat the trout fillets evenly with mustard. In a small bowl, combine the bread crumbs and herbs, and dredge the fillets in the crumb mixture. Melt the butter in a large skillet over medium heat, stirring occasionally until the butter browns slightly. Add the fish to the pan and fry for about 2 minutes on each side. Remove to a plate, and keep warm. Add the olive oil and garlic to the pan and sauté over high heat just until the garlic is fragrant. Add the spinach and toss to prevent the garlic from burning. Cook the spinach just until wilted, then season and transfer to a serving pan or plates as a bed for the trout fillets.

Tips, Tricks & Old-time Lore

• Before you head out, be sure to purchase a fishing license, and keep a copy of your state's fishing regulations handy. Both are available at bait and tackle shops, sporting-goods stores, and even some grocery stores and gas stations.

• When stream fishing with a bobber, sinker, and live bait, place the sinker about 9 inches above the hook. Place the bobber about 18 to 24 inches above the sinker. If you're fishing in deeper water, you may need to move the bobber further up the line from the sinker.

• A wine cork makes a fine bobber. Either poke a hole through it lengthwise with a needle, or slit it halfway through with your fillet knife and slide it onto your line.

• Fish are sensitive to smells, which can affect your catch, so dust your hands with baking soda or dirt before touching tackle to mask your human scent.

• When fishing with live bait, make your bait move as naturally as possible through the water.

• For flyfishers, lip balm is a cheap and effective alternative to floatant for coating your line.

• To freeze fish fillets, submerge them in a cardboard milk carton full of cold water, seal the carton, and freeze. This method helps prevent freezer burn and preserves the flavor of your catch.

• According to an old fish tale, you should spit on your bait if you expect to have any luck at all.

Best-bet Baits and Lures:
• Bass: minnows, spinners, jigs, flies
• Bluegill: crickets, flies
• Catfish: worms, frozen shrimp, stinky "prepared" baits
• Crappie: minnows, jigs
• Trout: worms, corn, Power Bait, salmon eggs, spinners, flies

"Having More Fun Than Anyone"

If you'd like to join a bona fide trail-blazing sisterhood, Sisters on the Fly awaits you. They're a growing group of women who caravan around the country in cute vintage trailers, fishing, running rivers, and having "more fun than anyone." They'll show you the ropes and spoil you rotten. Learn more at www.sistersonthefly.com .

Tools of the Trade

Fly Girl Rod (www.wright-mcgill.com)

Fly girl rods are designed from reel seat to tip specifically for the female fly caster, to fit a woman's hand. The 4-piece construction makes travel easy without sacrificing performance and strength. Made of birdseye maple reel seats and finished with a nickel/silver up-lock system, their fly rods include a beautiful and durable travel case trimmed in leather.

Cast AWAY

" *Fly fishing* is like raising children. You never know what's going to happen next. "

– Jimmy Moore

Shelley Bennett grew up in Moscow, Idaho, the daughter of a lumberjack who turned his enterprise into a logging empire. His strong work ethic passed to Shelley when she started her own real estate business as a single mother at age twenty-one. "It was always just take care of the kids and work, take care of the kids and work." Having sold her business recently, her yen to express her inner wild turned into a passion for fly fishing and trailer travel. "This is the first time I've given the gift of time back to myself."

Her '53 Aljoa trailer came into her life when her best friend,

Juli Thorson, saw it for sale in front of a fly-fishing shop. "I signed for the trailer then and there on Shelley's behalf and towed it to her house before she'd even laid eyes on it," Juli remembered. "It's that sharing-of-life-knowledge thing girlfriends do so well. Shelley helped me in equal measure when I was looking to buy my current horse ranch," said Juli, lifestyle editor for the magazine *Horse & Rider*.

"My grandchildren love to hit the road with me," Shelley says. "It's a way for this grown-up girl to play little-girl house again, fish, read, drink coffee, daydream."

Hooked
ON FASHION

Common fishing lures, available in most any sporting goods store, are the perfect statement for reel women "hooked" on fashion. At once "alluring," they come with names hilariously perfect for the gal who's got the urge! Hobby stores sell everything you need to turn fishing lures into earrings including beads to glue onto the ends of the barbed hooks. Be creative!

Cyclone ... he'll never know what hit him!
Pro-Glo Wedding Ring ... land a lunker!
Sparkle Tail ... 'nuf said?
Hook & Smile Blade ... wait until we're married!
Feel the Fight ... hooked on drama
Flutter ... heart-stopping
Stop & Go ... catch and release
Swinger ... multiple strikes

Have fun trolling! With a pair of alluring earrings, you'll have no problem reeling 'em in. For that next big catch, toss a line, then sink your hook into anything that nibbles. (Also on page 42, I've included plans for a lantern made from trolling gear, handy for the next time you need extra illumination while prowling.)

"Hooked"
ON
APRONS

My friend Juli Thorson and I have a "checkered past." Juli, lifestyle editor for *Horse & Rider* magazine, and I, an aproned neighbor, have plenty of apron tales to tell, some long, some pastel-colored, some bold, some faded, but all definitely checkered. It has to do with the year we both were born—1953. By the time we were twelve years old (Juli growing up on a farm in North Dakota), we had both cut and stitched our first aprons, in school, in church, in 4H, in Girl Scouts, with our grannies, aunties, and with our mothers. In rebuttal to those citified author types who claim to have rediscovered the apron, we started our collections almost from the cradle. We jokingly call our aprons "in vivo." They can't be retro if you've always worn them, made them, and collected them, right? In other words, we've been giving aprons a good "wrap" for over forty years.

Checkered gingham was our hands-down choice for apron duty. Unfortunately, gingham still has a bad rap amongst designer types—it's tacky, it's as common as burlap, and as "Madeline" and "Mildred" as, well, you know, the Agnes from Ohio jokes. But with the revival of aprons as kitchen couture, there's a new apron wearer, those for whom an apron is a statement of fashion. Fads come and go, but for women like Juli and me, it's a statement of attitude and practicality that others have yet to get hooked on, so to speak. Aprons are best kept by the back door, pockets full of hooks and moss—perfect for tossing in a few worms when you head to the creek for dinner, the way Juli does, at left—a good substitute for those "mannish" (and expensive) fishing vests.

Just as I've long made a case for the practical purpose of aprons, wearing them for construction, for fishing, for farming and more, I'm taking my stand in favor of gingham because when it comes to aprons, it's the perfect fabric. Since it comes with a pre-engineered grid, it's easy for a beginner to measure and cut. More important, it's easy to practice the stitching techniques you'll need to know once you start stitching in earnest—smocking, gathering, cross-stitching, rick rack applications, and more.

I have an image of my grandmother Artie that's forever etched in my memory. She's in a baggy house dress with huge pockets (another not-so-fashionable apron yet to be discovered), and she's working her way along a brushy creek bank. She's wearing flat-soled loafers and her legs are bare from the knees down. Her hair is in curlers and she's determined to catch us dinner. Little did she know, she was *way* ahead of the fashion curve, and still is! The way I figure it, aprons are capable of more than selling books. And urban discussions about the hostess aprons of the past keeping women in their place seem silly. We've always known our place—aproned up, and with a job that needs doing.

Juli Thorson was named for Juliana, the grandmother who appears in this travel scrapbook kept by her sister, Alvilde ("Toots"). Their car-camping trip, with two girlfriends, took place in the summer of 1929—in that golden window of "all things possible" just before the stock-market crash. The friends were all in their twenties, at the height of the flapper era. Juli's grandmother was a red-headed, born-independent child who didn't let the disapproval of others get in the way of pursuing adventure! Those of us who know Juli agree she inherited that independent side of her grandmother's personality.

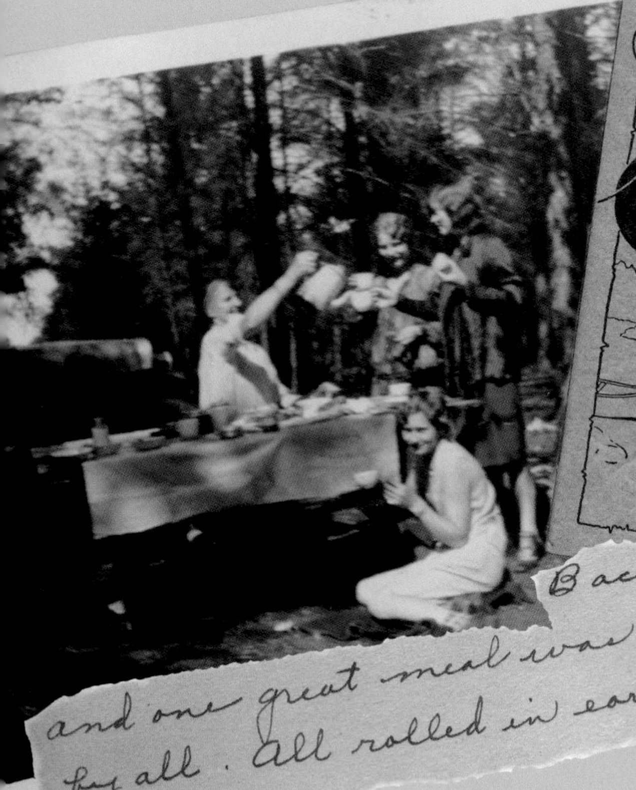

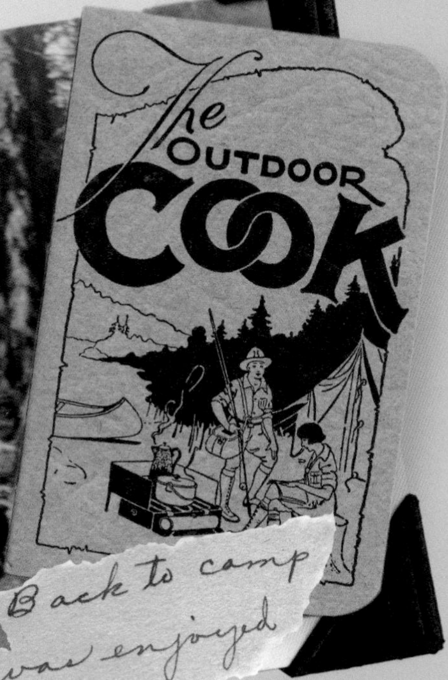

The OUTDOOR COOK

Back to camp and one great meal was enjoyed by all. All rolled in early.

MINNESOTA ARROWHEAD COUNTRY
fishing guide

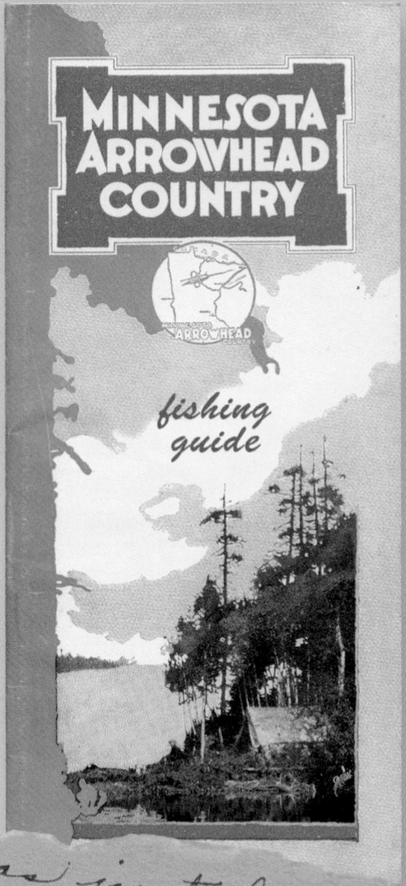

The water was just keen. Could camp here for a week its so nice.

104

This ticket entitles the holder to camp privileges for 24 hours at the

FOREST LAKE, MINNESOTA
Tourist Park
Charges 50c

Date July 22 1929
Hour 8 P. M.
Car No. ....
By N. H. KLOSTER, Marshall

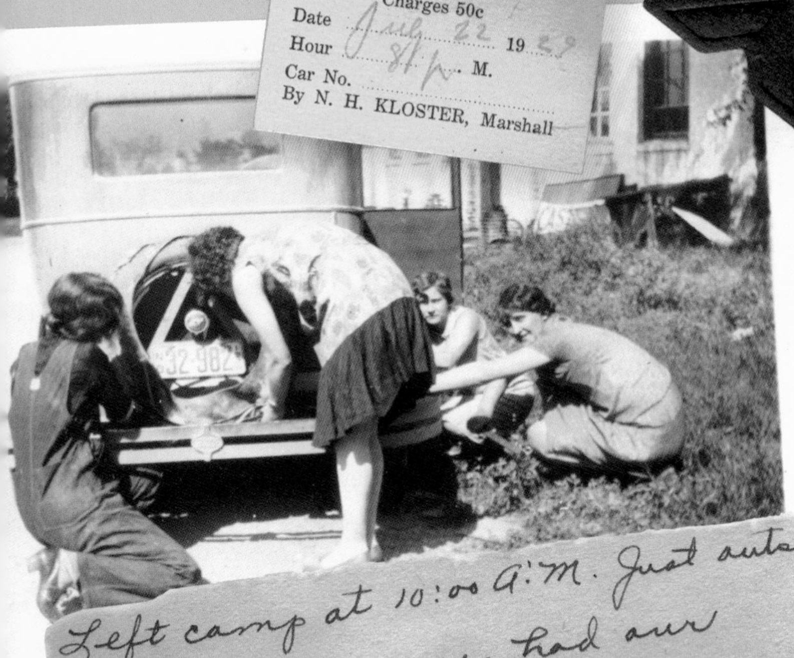

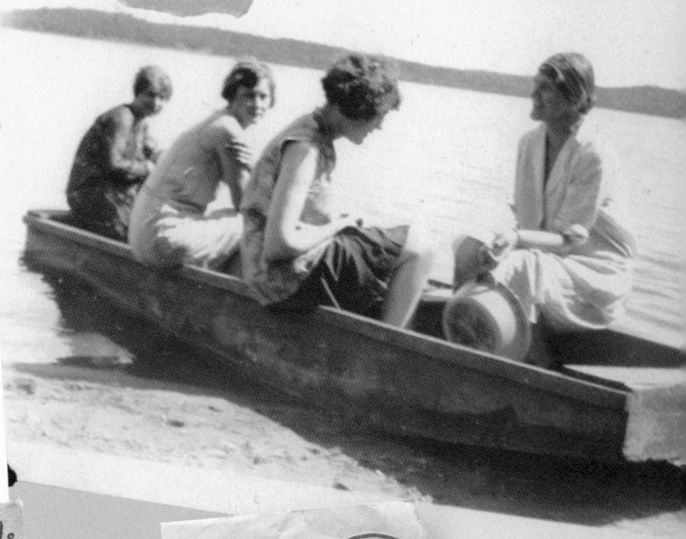

Left camp at 10:00 A.M. Just outside our tourist camp, we had our first flat tire. Put on our spare.

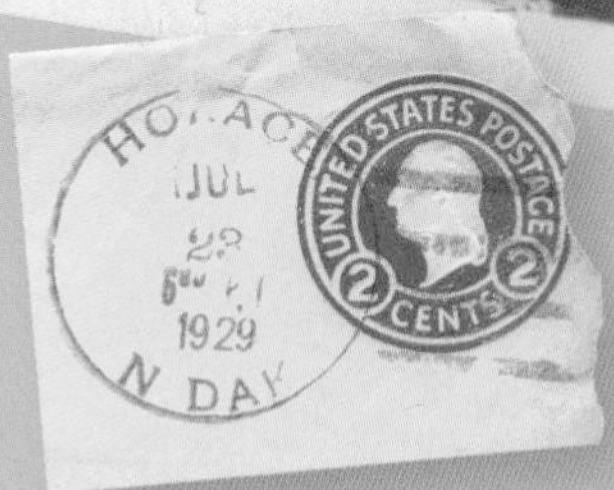

HORACE
JUL
23
1929
N DAK
UNITED STATES POSTAGE
2 CENTS 2

THE *Huntress*

When Taylor Valliant worked for me as an assistant graphics designer, she loved to dress up for work, occasionally even wearing her high heels to the farm. She liked to say, "If I can't dress up for work, where will I wear all my pretty clothes?" But when she married, moved to Montana, and had a baby, she also decided she'd like to hunt to provide her family with a healthy alternative to store-bought meat ... refusing to sit down and be just one thing!

Dear MaryJane,

I am reading Barbara Kingsolver's Animal, Vegetable, Miracle, and feel like I am really doing something important when I harvest my own meat raised by nature herself. I've had a couple of old Montana guys at the rifle range ask me why I decided to hunt, and I told them I was getting in touch with my feminine side and I also wanted to prove that a girl from Little Compton, Rhode Island, could hunt. But really, I want healthy organic meats for my family, and at the store, organic meats are expensive!

We are butchering our meat ourselves, so our only costs are the rifle, which will pay itself off rather quickly; ammunition; and a hunting license.

I had some interesting experiences when choosing a rifle to buy. I decided on a Ruger 30-06 because that's what the professionals at the gun store told me I should get. With that caliber you can hunt anything, and why limit yourself? But I was surprised how many people, even women, who were strangely unsupportive of this, saying I ought to have chosen a gun of a lesser caliber—the recoil was going to be too powerful. But I stuck to my guns (haha); after all, I carry around a 25-pound sack of "child" all day on my hip. Honestly, though, it doesn't bother me at all. When I've fired it out in the field, I noted, surprisingly, that I neither heard nor felt anything. I really felt one with my weapon.

I think that people are somehow intimidated by a woman that hunts, and this reflects on what type of gun they think we should use. I hear stories here all the time of wives who have bagged a deer before their husbands, only to have their husbands upset and jealous afterward (and these are "normal" guys behaving this way!). Although I have, for the most part, had overwhelming support. At the rifle range, the range-master spent over an hour teaching me the proper way to sight in a rifle for the first time. And my old friend Raven has been a big help. He grew up hunting in upstate New York and is an avid bowhunter. He came right over to show me how to hang, skin, and butcher my deer. When I told him I'd gotten some flack for getting such a small doe, his response was, "You can't eat antlers," and he made a point of complimenting me on how clean my field dressing was (learned from watching a video on the Internet, by the way).

It is a Native American ritual to eat the heart of an animal immediately after you kill it; that way its spirit will enter your body. Though I didn't eat it warm out of the body, I did prepare it for my helpers the night after the kill as a thank you. Here is the recipe. It is truly divine!

— Taylor

Venison Heart
APPETIZER

Clean the heart, cut it out of its sack, cut all tubes, and soak in salt water for up to 24 hours. Slice into thin strips and soak in 1 cup milk for 1-2 hours. Dredge strips in flour, dip back into milk, and roll in bread crumbs. Saute in oil until just done (be careful not to overcook). Serve on thin rounds of toasted French bread with melted brie cheese.

THE HUNT

NOW, AS A HUNDRED YEARS AGO,

women hunt

FOR THE SAME REASONS
MEN GENERALLY DO
and derive the same sorts of
satisfaction from hunting.
And regardless of the sex of the hunter,

every hunt

BEGINS WITH A STALK
AND ENDS WITH A STORY.

- Mary Zeiss Stange,
Heart Shots: Women Write About Hunting

Ithaca No 4
IN THE HANDS OF
MRS. E.B. BELKNAP

¶The best known amateur lady shot in the East.
¶Wife of an eminent physician who seems to think open air exercise better than pills.
¶Mrs. Belknap writes "Have had three other makes of guns and find my No. 4 Ithaca best of all".
¶Start your wife, daughter or sweetheart shooting and watch the roses come to her cheeks.

¶Featherweight guns especially for ladies.
¶Beautiful catalogue—FREE.
¶Eighteen grades guns—$17.75 net to $400 list

ITHACA GUN CO., DEPT. H. ITHACA, N.Y.

LOOKING BACK ...

Hunting was never a moral issue when I was a kid. It was a simple fact of life, an essential part of the equation that put food on our family dinner table. Spending money at grocery stores and restaurants wasn't an option when you didn't have the money. We were working-class poor, and that meant we relied on Mother Nature to fill our bellies. Along with what we raised—a huge garden, fruit trees, backyard chickens and rabbits—wild meat (fish included) sustained us. Little did I know how grateful I would be for having learned how to "scrape by" on the gifts of the land all these years later, driven not by finances now, but by the quest for the highest quality foods.

My parents taught me how to feed my family with skills that transcend shopping and commercial food production, and that all-natural upbringing fed me so heartily and so well that I have never known the kind

In the past fifty years, we Americans have all but lost touch with how meat gets from the field to our dinner tables. All of the packaging between us and what we consume buffers us from the notion that dirt, sweat, and blood have anything to do with it. Such table talk would be taboo in this age of grocery store harvesting and plastic-wrapped meals.

Industrial agriculture has stepped in to handle the messier aspects of growing and gathering the things we eat; all we have to do is pay for it, right? But we pay a much higher price than you might realize. Large-scale cattle, poultry, and swine operations, fueled by gasoline, pesticides, and chemical fertilizers, are gobbling up native landscapes and spitting out pastures primed for failure. Mile after mile of single-crop fields, planted to feed livestock, effectively wipe out the biodiversity that keeps ecosystems in balance, and when that balance is upset, plants and animals become vulnerable to pest infestations and disease. Humans intervene with chemical "remedies," and the situation only gets worse. Our nation's soils are losing their structure, nutrients, and microorganisms so that, over time, countless acres are withering into unproductive wastelands and eroding into our waterways along with toxic byproducts. Plus, much of the meat produced in this way travels a thousand miles or more to reach the consumer, chugging fossil fuels and spewing pollution the whole way.

So what can we do to address this destructive practice on a personal level? Enter the "eat local" revolution. In an effort to right the innumerable wrongs of the industrial agricultural system, more people are seeking out food as close to home as possible. This way, they know what they're getting and how their local environment is affected by their choices. This may be a new-fangled idea to some, but hunters have known it all along.

Venturing out into nearby woodlands in pursuit of wild game is the original definition of "eating local." As a species we are naturally omnivorous, meaning we are built to eat plants and meat, so we have a legitimate place among the ranks of native predators. Like our carnivorous four-legged counterparts, we have subsisted on wild quarry for centuries. When practiced in a responsible manner, hunting is a sustainable tool that balances prey populations with habitat. The absence of human hunters, coupled with sparse wild predator populations, would result in prey populations that overwhelm the available resources and ultimately suffer from starvation or disease. Not to mention, there is ecological justice in eating meat from an animal that eats naturally from the land. No crops, no chemicals, no pollutants, no soil erosion.

As humans, though, hunting does require an up-close-and-personal acknowledgment that meat comes from sentient living creatures. It's easy to ignore the fact that industrial farming results in the inhumane slaughter of millions of animals each year, but a hunter meets her quarry one-on-one. Yet, even as we cringe at

of nutritional famine that plagues many Americans. There is genuine satisfaction in knowing how to sow a seed and, as a meat eater, how to kill an animal with merciful efficiency.

My induction into the ways of "eating wild" came early on, and it was an intoxicating experience. Each fall, my entire Mormon clan took to the sagebrush flats of Utah for two weeks in order to live deliberately with a single mission: to bring home food. Like a nomadic tribe, we set up camp, slept on the ground, and swiftly fell into wild ways with natural grace. For us kids, deer camp was the seasonal getaway we dreamed of throughout the rest of the year, especially since our parents took us out of school. We had serious responsibilities— gathering firewood, fetching water, and washing clothes—but somehow there was an exhilarating freedom in working hard for the sake of survival, especially when we woke up covered in snow. When we weren't helping out, we were free to explore, discover, and wonder—Tom Sawyer and Huck Finn had nothing on us.

When the "adult" hunters (men and women age fourteen and older) began bringing in deer, we gathered with the primal joy of coyotes or wolves. Each harvested animal promised delicious food throughout the winter. Not only would we eat, we would savor. Early on, I learned how to field dress a deer, the process of transforming a living creature into precious food. I watched as the adults, with clear purpose, promptly cleaned, hung, and wrapped each carcass, and we rejoiced in our bounty by eating the heart, liver, and choicest cuts. Pan-fried over the campfire, it was the best meat imaginable. Afterward, my cousins,

Mary Jane, Kent, and Scott, 1957

brothers, and I would hop up and resume our play with the blood and spirit of wild things coursing through us.

Today, I continue to thrive on the energy of protein eaten straight from the land. Why eat legumes and grains grown in soil that was tilled by a tractor fueled by petroleum, a process that hijacks the very essence of wild animals, their habitat? I've decided that if I want to promote wild over domesticated, I must commit to eating wild whenever possible.

This past hunting season, my husband shot an elk in the woods not far from our back door (one of the luxuries of outpost living), and likewise my son-in-law harvested his first deer. Memories of being a wild child at deer camp flooded back to me—the smell of hide, the work of separating meat from bone, the hours of wrapping and packaging, the process of turning certain cuts into jerky, and the gratification of feeding ourselves. Filling a shopping cart doesn't feel nearly as conscious and sustainable as filling my granddaughter's bowl with elk stew.

66 *On some deep level* beneath civility or compassion, I am exhilarated by the pursuit of wild and wary prey. I have found a place within the circle. Here among the animals, guilt is of no consequence, and there is no such thing as sin.

– Jennifer Bové, *A Place Among Elk*

the thought of actually killing something, we've got to recognize that our primal purpose is to do just that. There is a certain deep fulfillment in harvesting food for yourself, whether it's the huckleberry or the deer. In his acclaimed book *The Omnivore's Dilemma*, Michael Pollan explains it in terms of accountability. Learning to eat from the wild, he says, gave him "the opportunity, so rare in modern life, to eat in full consciousness of everything involved in feeding myself: For once, I was able to pay the full karmic price of a meal."

Scott, Mary Jane, Scottie, and Kent, 1958

Ask any hunter, and she'll tell you that hunting invokes a very personal sense of stewardship for all natural resources. Hunters relish time spent in the wild, on the ground, observing the intricate workings of nature. More than mere visitors to the outdoors, they're often more at home in the woods than in their own living rooms. They understand the interconnectedness of the ecosystems that feed their families and nourish their spirits. In short, hunters have a deep emotional investment in their surroundings, and that translates into a conscientious ecological investment as well.

Hunters are often referred to as the original conservationists because of their commitment to preserving wildlife and wild lands. Beyond hunting license fees and charitable donations, they also support The Federal Aid in Wildlife Restoration Act, passed by Congress in 1937 to impose a federal excise tax on

hunting equipment. Money generated by the tax funds habitat improvement, wildlife management research, education, hunter training, and public target ranges. All outdoor enthusiasts, from hunters to hikers, benefit from this tax, but hunters willingly foot the bill.

Understanding a hunter's passion requires that one experience nature from a gut-level perspective. All the cerebral controversy that surrounds hunting occurs outside the realm of sunrise and frost-tinged leaves, scents of wild musk, tracks on a stream bank, and chilly toes. These are the treasures of the hunt, as are solitude, patience, the heart-pounding thrill of a wild animal's approach, the satisfaction of a swift merciful kill, and precious meat to bring home.

The Greek goddess Artemis was revered as the goddess of both hunting and childbirth. She symbolized the primeval cycle from life to death, and the seamless transition from one to the other. Perhaps it is this cyclical dance, almost feminine in nature, that draws women to hunt. Whether they begin hunting on a man's coattails or seek it out on their own, women are now hunting in record numbers. A 2005 study by the National Sporting Goods Association estimated that more than 3 million women hunt, accounting for about 16 percent of the nearly 21 million active hunters in the United States. According to the study, 2.4 million women hunted with firearms in 2005, up 72 percent from 2001, and the number of women bow-hunters has grown 176 percent to 786,000. Clearly, intrepid women are driven to get back in touch with what they eat and what they feed their families, and those who hunt are reclaiming their place in the wild.

OUTSPOKEN...

Erica Hill, a central Missouri hunter, killed this big white-tailed buck with her .30-30 rifle in the fall of 2006. Although she started hunting to share a common interest with her husband, she now enjoys going solo. "I just love being out in the woods, watching and listening to nature," she says. Erica hunts with both rifle and bow, but she prefers the intimacy of archery. "It takes a lot of skill to get within bow range of a deer, and it's exciting to interact with a wild animal so closely." Erica firmly believes that more women should take up hunting. "It's empowering to tough out those cold, dark hours before sunrise and come home with food for your family."

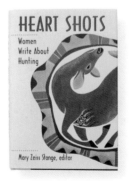

Heart Shots:
Women Write About Hunting
by Mary Zeiss Stange
Offering an eloquent array of original short stories and novel excerpts, this collection illuminates women's intuitive approach to nature and hunting throughout modern history.

Butters clan harvesting deer, 1960

Birding

In 1962, Rachel Carson warned us that manmade materials would adversely impact our bird populations, and someday could result in a world without birdsong—a "Silent Spring." Some forty years later, I found this nest at my farm—woven throughout it are strands of white plastic found somewhere—of course, nowhere on my property.

CARSON

Silent Spring

SILENT SPRING

WITH AN INTRODUCTION BY VICE PRESIDENT *Al Gore*

RACHEL CARSON

Birders are an avid breed of hunter, but they aren't out to kill. Armed with binoculars, cameras, and field guides, they venture into creekbeds and thickets in hopes of stealing a glimpse—or better yet, a photo—of rare or unusual birds.

In temperate regions, spring and fall migrations bring the best variety of bird life, and early morning is typically the best time of the day to view birds as they're busy feeding. Competitive birders known as "listers" are bent on spotting as many species as possible, keeping lists of sightings as they go. But as more and more birders delve into the wilds, there is growing concern about their impact on birds and habitat. Birding etiquette is evolving to maintain the integrity of one of the fastest growing outdoor pursuits in America. To minimize stress on birds, conscientious birders limit photography and sound recording, and they keep their distance from nests.

Visit the National Audubon Society (www.audubon.org) and the American Birding Association (www.americanbirding.org) to learn more about birding and related conservation efforts.

OUTSPOKEN...

Ecologist Rachel Carson boldly pioneered the modern environmental movement with the publication of her most famous book, *Silent Spring*, in 1962. Alarmed by the rampant use of synthetic pesticides after World War II, Carson set out to challenge industrial agricultural and government policy. In plain-spoken language, *Silent Spring* exposed widespread ecological degradation due to human negligence, and it spurred a revolution of environmental consciousness. Carson also argued that for the first time in history, people were being exposed to chemicals that could wreak long-term havoc on their health. She blamed the pesticide DDT for declines in certain bird populations and warned that continued use of DDT would one day result in a spring without birdsong—a "silent spring."

Not surprisingly, the chemical industry retaliated, claiming Carson was hysterically trying to thwart the nation's "progress." But Carson would not fold, and her perseverance had lasting impact. Citing *Silent Spring*, the Kennedy administration ordered a study on the effects of pesticides, ultimately resulting in a ban on DDT. And Carson testified before Congress in 1963 in support of a federal department that would study human and environment health. Seven years later, the Environmental Protection Agency was established.

Rachel Carson died in 1964 after a long battle with breast cancer, but her wisdom continues to educate and inspire appreciation for the world around us.

Nesting

When spring arrives, I bolt out my door looking for abandoned bird nests that have fallen to the ground. My collection dates back to a time before I was a sitting, brooding, nesting mother. Tucking my collection of nests away in boxes didn't seem right. Putting them on a shelf didn't work either, so I created a year-round display on branches. I can even hang other treasures on them.

If you're looking for a reason to get outside, try a nesting and twigging expedition. Prowling a mall might satiate the same urge, but outside the air is cleaner and the decorative goods you bring home are free. If you venture near a barnyard, you might find a nest made entirely from horsehair. Near a bog, you might find a soft, fluffy nest built from the cotton of a cattail. If you're in sagebrush country, watch for nests made from shredded sage bark. In a forest, look for mossy nests.

The next time someone questions your need to fuss at home, say you're gathering essentials for a nurturing nest and you simply can't help yourself. The next time you spend an evening with the bathroom door locked, steaming every pore, call it preening. Like our feathered friends, we flutter about building and shaping our homes. We flap and fret. We satiate our urge with baskets, ginghams, and colors. We nesters know our designing is more than lighting, flooring, fabric, and paint.

Kids...
BEYOND THE BACKYARD

" It seems to me that *we all look at Nature too much, and live with her too little.* "

– Oscar Wilde

Preparation and Patience

The foundation of any fun outing with kids is mom's mindset. You've got to schedule the time to go, whether for one hour or several days, then resolve to live without a schedule. Too many expectations and goals are sure to be derailed by the whims of childhood, so leave your day planner at home. Kids are natural-born experts at smelling roses, spying bugs, and digging in the dirt, and while their agenda may seem slow and tedious to us grown-ups, it's important that we allow them the freedom to explore at their own pace. Dragging them from one "exciting" activity to the next is a sure way to turn them off to the pleasures of the outdoors.

A flexible sense of adventure is easier to accomplish, though, if the big stuff is planned out in advance. That means deciding when to set out, where you'll go, and what you need to bring.

Take a Child Outside

With the growing awareness that kids (and their parents) need more outside time, it's becoming easier to find ideas, information, and inspiration. In fact, the North Carolina Museum of Natural Sciences is building a comprehensive website of resources for outbound families across the country.

Explore www.takeachildoutside.org, where you can:

• pledge to take a child outside
• find a list of interesting outdoor activities nationwide
• find participating organizations in your area
• record your outdoor experiences

Weather (or not) to Go

Before heading out beyond your backyard, be sure to consult one authority besides your calendar: the weather forecast. Weather is the boss out there, and you've got to behave according to her rules (especially when you've got kids in tow). Looking out the window isn't gonna cut it either. Up in the mountains, a snowstorm can sideswipe you in July, and down south, a summer deluge can swamp the best-laid plans.

The National Weather Service has a fantastic website (www.nws.noaa.gov) where you can get the lowdown on Mother Nature's moods. If I want to head out for a hike with my granddaughter, for example, I can pull up the NWS website, type in "Moscow, ID," and get the seven-day forecast for my area. Plus, there's a "clickable" map that allows me to zone in or expand my search. That way, I can target both the best day and the best location for our outing. In your neck of the woods, you might also be interested in tidal charts, snow cover, and river levels.

Finding the Perfect Place to Play

If you're a seasoned outdoorswoman, you've already got a pretty good feel for the lay of the land within reasonable driving distance from your house. "Reasonable," of course, depends on your family's own tolerance level, but under an hour is usually a good rule of thumb. You don't want to wear out the kids before the adventure even begins.

If you're new at this and aren't sure where to find a good, safe spot, consider starting with a state park, national monument, or national historic site. These areas usually offer nicely maintained trails and educational centers within a natural setting. Other options include national forests, wildlife refuges, state wildlife or conservation areas, and state forests. Even city parks often have green space and a creek to splash around in.

Time to gather up some resources to fuel your backroads brainstorm!

Researching Destinations Online

Let's say you're living in Joplin, Missouri, and you don't want to be in your car with your toddler for more than twenty minutes. How do you find the perfect place for a day hike and picnic?

First, check out MapQuest online (www.mapquest.com) and watch the world unfold at your fingertips!

If you search a general place name like "state park" near your town, you'll get a list of options complete with addresses, phone numbers, and driving distances. Plus, each option will show up on a map so you can see where it's situated relative to your home base.

Hmmmm … looks like the only state park is Crawford State Park in Pittsburg, Kansas, about twenty-five miles away. If you have to stop for gas or directions, twenty-five miles may be pushing your time limit. So, try again for something closer. Searching "national monument" turns up Carver National Monument only twelve miles to the southeast. Looks good at a glance, but what kind of place is it really?

" Between every two pines is a doorway to a new world."

– John Muir

MARYJANESFARM® OUTPOST

APPROXIMATE VAR 11°00E (1989) FOUNDED TO THE NEAREST HALF DEGREE

MOSCOW USA

116°58'00"W

46°40'30"N

To feel out a spot before I go, one of my favorite resources is GORP (the Great Outdoor Recreation Pages), http://gorp.away.com. GORP has the goods on almost any outdoor destination imaginable. You can search destinations far and wide based on what kinds of activities you're interested in as well as the "family-friendliness" factor.

Here's what GORP has to say about Carver National Monument (sounds like this place offers everything you need to have a safe, fun, and fascinating adventure!):

George Washington Carver National Monument

George Washington Carver National Monument was established in 1943 as a public memorial to George Washington Carver in recognition of his outstanding achievements as a scientist, educator, and humanitarian. Although Dr. Carver spent only 10 to 12 years on the Diamond Grove Farm, the area and community greatly influenced the course of his life. It was here that Carver was born into slavery and orphaned as an infant. Yet, he grew up with a love and appreciation of nature that would sustain him throughout his life. The park consists of 210 of the original 240-acre Moses Carver Farm.

• Operating Hours: The park is open daily from 9 a.m. until 5 p.m. Closed Thanksgiving, Christmas, and New Year's Day. Mild to cold weather in the winter. Summers are generally hot and humid.

• Visitor Center/Exhibits/Programs: The visitor center includes a museum, bookstore, and films on George Washington Carver's life.

• Trails, Roads: Outside the visitor center is the 3/4-mile Carver Trail (walking trail) which winds its way through woodlands and tall grass prairie. Along this trail you can see the Carver Birthplace Site, Carver Boyhood Statue, Carver Spring, Williams Pond and Spring, Moses Carver 1881 House, and Carver Family Cemetery. The trail is only partially handicapped accessible.

• Lodging and camping facilities: None in the park. A variety of hotels, motels, and RV/camping sites are available in the surrounding area.

• Accessibility: Picnic area, comfort station, wheelchair accessible to visitor center, and a wheelchair is available on request.

• Special Events/Programs: Ranger programs are presented at 10 a.m. and 2 p.m. daily during peak months. There are special programs offered by staff and/or volunteers throughout the year. Special events include: African-American Month, February; Women's History Month, March; March for Parks, April; Airing of the Quilts, June; Carver Day, July; National Parks Month, August; Prairie Day and GEM City Days, September; Native-American Month and Miracle March, November; Holiday Open House, December.

The Bové Family in the Wild

My friendship with outdoor writer Jennifer Bové was forged by fire, campfire that is. We met in 2004 when Jen invited me to contribute an essay to her anthology *A Mile in Her Boots*. That summer, she came out to my farm to visit, and we sat around the fire swapping tales about our early days working in the wilderness.

Jen has a bunch of backcountry adventures under her belt. She has mucked around Ozark sloughs netting fish, snorkeled chilly Northwest rivers counting salmon, and waded wetlands in search of sandhill cranes. She and her husband Chris even lived on a remote island wildlife refuge for a year, where their only neighbors were seabirds and elephant seals. But if you ask her, she'll tell you that none of her wild work compares to her current job as mother of three youngsters: Rita, Sophie, and Sam.

"When Chris and I set out into the uncharted territory of parenthood," she says, "neither of us was ready to give up the 'wild life,' so we had to figure out how our kids could come along."

Somehow, Jen manages to make it look easy. Her family has been hiking, canoeing, camping, and fishing from

Low-tech Trip Planning

Okay, but what if you're new to, say, Missoula, Montana, and you don't have Internet service hooked up yet? Your preteen sons are itching to get out and try trout fishing in the Bitterroot River, but you don't want to drive around all day searching for a public access.

No trouble. Get out your phone book and flip to the "Community" or "Recreation" pages. These unsung guides are often chock full of information about local parks, trails, campgrounds, and, yes, fishing accesses.

If you don't find what you need there, skip over to the "Government Listings" section (often edged in blue). Under state agencies, you'll find a phone number for the local Fish and Game Department. Call 'em up and pick their brains for ideas (have a pencil and paper ready to scratch down directions).

Within a five-minute conversation, you'll find out that the Chief Looking Glass fishing site is a nice spot with plenty of bank-fishing access, shade trees, bathrooms, and picnic tables. It's only fourteen miles south of Missoula, and on your way there, you can stop by Wal-Mart to get your Montana Conservation License ($8) and a fishing permit ($15). The kids fish for free.

Who knows, the person you talk to might even fess up to specific lures, flies, or bait the fish are biting this time of year. Never hurts to ask!

Kid Gear: What You Need and Where to Get It

Clothing

There's no reason to go broke outfitting your kids for the outdoors, but they do need climate-appropriate clothing. If you're well into the heat of summer with no chance of being caught in a cold snap, clothing is not much of a concern. At the creek, kids are often happiest running around without a stitch on, and who can blame them? Just keep them slathered in sunscreen (and a big-brimmed hat, if they'll keep it on), and remember that moist bottoms sitting in the sand can become irritated, so provide a towel or encourage undies. Also make sure they've got a T-shirt and pants if you'll be hiking out through poison ivy, nettles, or thorns.

In cold weather, or those unpredictable spring and fall months, it's better to be prepared with a layering system. If you're just taking a short walk in the park, jeans and flannels are fine. But, if you're camping or hiking for more than an hour or so, new-fangled fibers offer comfort and safety. Depending on conditions, bundle your babe in one or more of the following layers:

1. Base Layer: Long or short-sleeved synthetic T-shirt and pants. Synthetic fibers, like polyester, wick sweat away from the skin and dry quickly, unlike cotton, which holds moisture and can result in a seriously cold kid.

2. Middle Layer: Fleece or down jacket to retain body heat, and fleece pants if it's really chilly.

3. Outer Layer: Waterproof nylon jacket (with a hood) and pants or overalls. Even if it's too warm to wear these items, pack them along on extended outings. This layer is a lifesaver when it comes to wind, rain, or snow. And don't forget a fleece stocking cap and two pairs of mittens: fleece under waterproof nylon.

Footwear

Kids often get cheated on shoes because they grow out of them quickly and rarely complain about discomfort while trying them on at the store. But, when hiking for miles and scrambling over rough terrain, little feet deserve quality and care.

For summer, I recommend a good pair of sandals for hot-weather hikes and water play. No flip-flops; I'm talking the kind with sturdy, padded straps that secure the foot on a solid rubber sole. For cooler weather, invest in a pair of boots or shoes equipped with lugged soles for traction, leather uppers, and ankle support. Let your kids run around in their boots for at least a couple of weeks to break them in before testing them on the trail. In winter, tuck those tootsies into waterproof snow boots. Look for thick, cushy liners that pull out for thorough drying.

As far as socks go, opt for one or two synthetic pairs to wear under hiking and snow boots (again, moisture wicking is critical, so NO cotton). Smartwool and Thorlo are both top brands.

Kid Carriers

There are all kinds of kid carriers on the market these days, but you've got to be on the lookout for characteristics that equal comfort for you and your little rider. Whether you need a front pack (for carrying a newborn against your chest) or a backpack (for babies six months and older), look for padded shoulder straps, a padded waist belt, adjustment points, and harness straps for securing baby. Don't skimp—those one-shoulder "sling" carriers and basic models without waist belts are not designed for hiking. Instead, opt for higher-tech packs such as those created by Kelty, Sherpani, and Deuter. There are a lot of neat accessories available too: sun/rain guards, stirrups, zip-on compartments, and so on.

the beginning, but their eyes really light up when they talk about elk hunting.

"For three years running, we've reserved at least one long week in September to escape to the mountains. We pack warm clothes, tons of food, archery equipment, and our dogs—and we just do it!"

Jen enjoys being the "den mother" around camp while Chris goes hunting, often with their daughters in tow.

"Out in the woods, we can allow our kids a rare kind of freedom and nurture their love of nature."

"Wild parenting," as Jen calls it, can give you blisters, bruises, and blazing headaches. But, as a whole, it's such a rewarding lifestyle that she wouldn't trade it for anything easier. She admits she's still learning the ropes, but she has learned a few important lessons along the way:

Wild with Child Tips for Backpacking with Kids

- Pack more snacks than you think you'll need: fruit, veggies and dip, almonds, cheese, whole-grain crackers and cookies, granola, and jerky are fuel for fun.
- Assign jobs. Whether it's gathering sticks for a campfire, cleaning a fish, or pitching the tent, kids will relish the responsibility.
- Remember this: "God made dirt; dirt don't hurt."
- Boost your kids' confidence, even when the chips are down, and you'll foster their identity as outdoor people.
- When it comes to environmental ethics, lead by example. Seeing you pick up trash is way more inspiring than listening to a lecture about it.
- Sometimes, when the going gets tough, the tough pack up and go home—and that's okay.

Visit Jennifer at *The View From My Boots*, www.bovesboots.blogspot.com.

Strollers

If you're packing your baby or toddler, you really don't need a stroller. But, if you prefer to keep the weight off your back, jog strollers are a convenient way to tote your little passenger and extras like food and jackets. Kelty, BOB, and InStep brand strollers are maneuverable, portable, and trail-tough. They have suspension systems far superior to the old umbrella strollers and chunky tires that cushion kids over bumps and vibrations. Most models collapse into handy storage size and even the double-passenger models are light enough to haul easily in and out of your car.

Where to Buy

Upside Over is a growing parent-run company that strives to offer the best possible outdoor gear and information to adventurous families. Their web-based store (www.upsideover.com), covers all the bases, from clothing to all-terrain strollers to first aid kits.

A number of other outdoor gear retailers like Patagonia, REI, and Cabelas also offer extensive lines of kid gear, but if you're looking for big discounts on quality products, try the Kids' Corner at Sierra Trading Post (www.sierratradingpost.com). Sierra sells name brand overstocks and closeouts, passing savings of 35 to 70 percent on to customers.

Bringing Baby

Having a wee one is no reason to stay cooped up indoors. Babies benefit from open skies as much as new parents do. With a bit of preparation, you can safely strike out with your infant. After all, our ancestors were packing their newborns around the wilderness thousands of years ago, long before cell phones and fleece buntings.

Safety Note:

Keep in mind that babies lose body heat quickly; they can become dangerously chilled even when you're warm from exertion. Bring more warm clothing than you think you'll need in case of spills and diaper leaks. Also, they are susceptible to dehydration as well as sunburn and wind chapping, and they may not fuss until they're in real trouble. Be diligent—check your little one often and adjust clothing, shade, etc., as needed.

Feeding

Breast milk is the perfect food for active moms and babes, hands-down. But if you bottle feed, you'll need to plan out how much formula and how many bottles you'll need to cover your excursion. When baby reaches the solid food stage, simply feed her as you would at home. Since jars of baby food are heavy, keep them to a minimum and just feed mashed, unsalted versions of your own meals.

Feeding tip: If your kid pack has a sturdy stand-alone frame, you can use it like a high chair—it keeps baby upright and your hands free while feeding!

Diapering

The idea of diapering needn't incite panic when planning an outdoor trip. Figure out how many diapers you'll need by counting your baby's daily diaper usage at home, and then bring extras.

Whether you use cloth or disposables, follow the "pack it in, pack it out" mantra. Under no circumstance should you bury or burn diapers. When my kids were young, cloth rested easier on my conscience because I was toting laundry home, not trash.

Cloth Diaper Duty Made Simple:

• Scrape poop into a hole, just like you'd dig for yourself.
• Whenever possible, lay diapers and diaper covers out on a branch or nylon clothesline to dry in the sun. Dry diapers are lighter to carry than wet ones and are less likely to mold. (Cloth diapers dry; disposables don't.)
• Store dirty diapers and cloth wipes in sealed plastic bags. Remember, in bear country smelly diapers should be treated with the same care as food and other attractants.
• If you run low on diapers and need to wash them, go downstream from your water source or fill a container with water. Soak the diapers for a few minutes, and then use a biodegradable soap such as Dr. Bronner's Natural Castile Soap to wash them, folding each in half to scrub one side of the cotton prefold against the other. Make sure you rinse out the soap completely in fresh water. Hang dry your diapers with any stains facing toward the sun for "sun-bleaching." Sunlight will sterilize your diapers as they dry.
• Good sanitation is a must. Wash hands with Dr. Bronner's soap or use antibacterial hand cleaner after handling dirty diapers.
• Also consider your baby's tender bum. Sitting in a pack for long periods can lead to diaper rash, so make sure to change diapers regularly, keep the skin clean, and allow as much open-air exposure as possible.

Carrying On ...

That's me above with daughter Meg in the Selway-Bitterroot Wilderness area, 1980 (I carried her on a fifty-four-mile hike!). Below, Meg hikes with her baby StellaJane along those same trails, 2007.

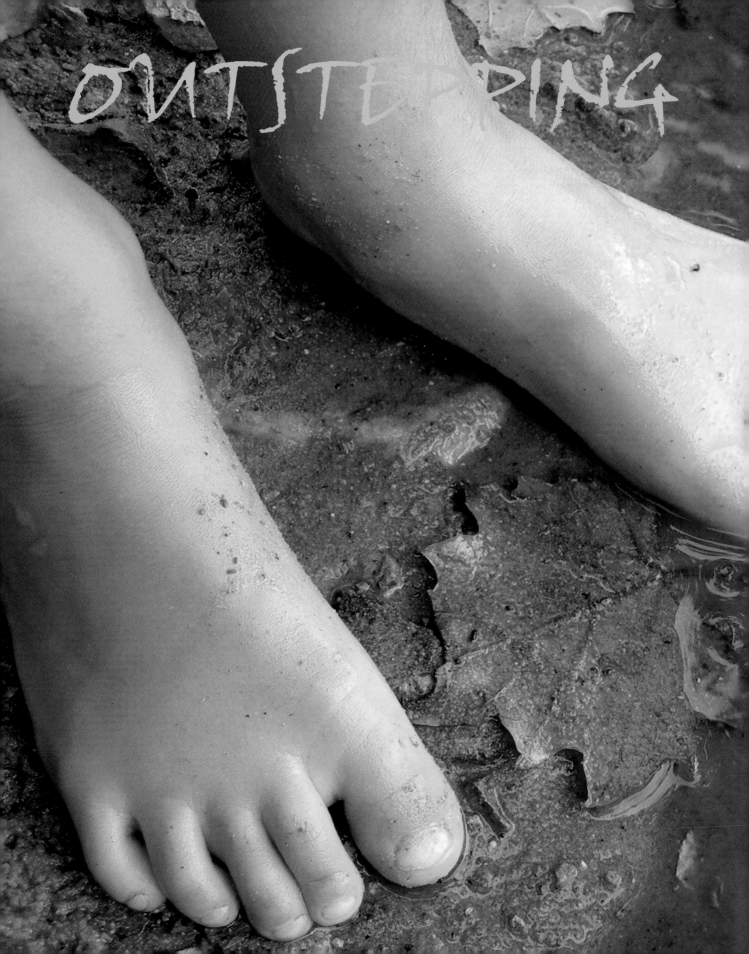

OUTSTEPPING

Gearing Up, HEADING OUT

"We need **the tonic of wildness,** to wade sometimes in marshes where the bittern and the meadow-hen lurk; to smell the whispering sedge where only the wilder and more solitary fowl builds her nest, and the mink crawls with its belly close to the ground."

– Henry David Thoreau

IN THIS CHAPTER

HEADING OUT

Exploring High Mountain Lakes in the Rockies
A story of their ecology and natural history

Fred W. Rabe

The crunch of dry sage roots under boot soles. The heady scent of pine. Lavender sky, early evening chill, legs pumped from all those miles behind you. You approach a thicket of willows that veils the creek and its secret springs, warm and waiting. At last. You shoulder through the willows with only a passing thought of moose or bear, loosening the sweat-soaked green bandanna from your head as you go. On the other side, granite walls loom, and you feel as if you've entered a lost world, a place untouched, a place where you're hidden from all the eyes of the world.

Here, where jewel-toned pebbles reflect the last light of day, you release your pack and ease its weight to the ground. Without so much as a glance over your shoulder, you shed shoes, shorts, shirt, and the rest—dropping them in a careless pile. The water beckons, both seductive and safe. As the sun slips down the canyon wall, setting the willows ablaze, you slip into the pool and melt. This is why you pushed your muscles to the limit today. This is why you came. To bathe—or rather to be bathed—in water that is not only warm and clear, but wild. This water, which courses up from a deep vein in the earth, seems to wash away all pretense, leaving you pure and whole.

Before dark, you will emerge renewed, kindle up a small fire, and cook a simple meal. You will lie down to sleep on the ground, in the chill open air, because tonight the tent just feels too . . . constricting. You will trace the constellations with your eyes until you drift off toward morning, toward another day on the trail.

Isn't that why we hunger to get out there with only a pack full of belongings? Backpacking allows us to fall into natural rhythms as we seek a deeper sense of ourselves. We can leave the cluttered "everyday" behind for awhile and rediscover the stuff that matters (it is so sweet to remember that the blackberry was a wild fruit to be savored off the vine before it became a must-have electronic gadget!). We find space, time, and quiet in the wild. We find refuge where we can bare body and soul. And maybe most rewarding of all, when we are forced to rely on our basic survival instincts, we are reminded in no uncertain terms that yes, indeed, we can.

One of the treats I allow myself when I go backpacking is at least one book packed with the kinds of facts that make me appreciate the landscape I'm experiencing in a much deeper way. More than travel guides, books like Fred Rabe's *Exploring High Mountain Lakes in the Rockies* take you beyond the surface of a geographic feature such as a lake or an outcropping.

With the extra time on your hands, you learn about things like *benthos*, organisms living on the bottom of lakes; *circuli*, growth rings on the scales of fish; *krummholz*, stunted growth of conifers near or at timberline; *tarn*, small mountain lakes; and *scree*, debris lying on a slope.

You can make up riddles as you walk to keep your mind off the miles ahead. "Darn that tarn full of benthos surrounded by krummholz seriously lacking in circuli. Scree it."

If you really had some time on your hands, you could challenge yourself to write a book like "1,000 Miles in the Rockies Before You Die" using Fred's book that takes you 1,000 miles from a lake that straddles the border of Canada and Idaho to a waterbody in New Mexico's Sangre de Cristo Range. Ambitious? Fred did it. Roughly 8,000 mountain lakes are nestled in the Rocky Mountains, representing one of the most pristine ecosystems in the country. "Tarn"ation, what are you waiting for?

Calculating Your Carbon Footprint

Despite our best intentions to live by the mantra "take only photos, leave only footprints," our carbon footprint is not an easy one for the Earth to erase.

What is a carbon footprint? It's the amount of greenhouse gasses produced by human activities such as driving a car or using electricity, measured in units of carbon dioxide gas (CO_2). You can assess your own personal CO_2 output and its impact on global warming using free online calculators such as those at Carbon Footprint (www.carbonfootprint.com) and An Inconvenient Truth (www.climatecrisis.net/takeaction/carboncalculator).

Sounds grim, but the good news is that there are ways to reduce and offset your CO_2 contribution so that you become "carbon neutral." Carpooling, public transportation, and buying local goods are all great ways to reduce gasoline usage, and there are lots of ways to cut down on electricity: hanging clothes out to dry, washing dishes by hand, and equipping light fixtures with energy efficient bulbs are just a few ideas. But you may want to go the extra mile and purchase "carbon offsets" for yourself, your business, or as gifts to compensate for unavoidable CO_2 pollution. At my farm, we purchase renewable energy for our headquarters and food production facility.

Choosing a Pack

The memory of hefting around the wrong backpack is etched upon my shoulders for life. In my early twenties, I was hired as one of the first female wilderness rangers for the U.S. Forest Service, and the only pack I'd been able to scrounge up for the job was an oversized external-frame Kelty. I packed it to the gills, seduced by all the room inside, and I ended up hefting half my body weight in a pack made for a man's broad build.

Today, there are so many outstanding options, from day packs to long-haul internal frame packs, that you can hardly go wrong. Still, there are a few components to check out when searching for that perfect pack.

Look for:

• Shoulder straps that bend without big creases that might rub uncomfortably while on the trail.
• A wide, thick, sturdy foam hip belt for proper support. Too-soft foam will mush and slide down your hips; too rigid can bruise. Make sure it cups over your hipbones to spread out the weight-bearing surface area.
• A back panel allows air flow and keeps your back cool.
• A zipper to access the main compartment (a full "horseshoe" zipper allows easiest access).
• Minimal extra pockets. Lots of external compartments add weight and bulk. One extra pocket along with a couple of loops and lash points are all you need.
• Adjustable fit (appropriate pack size for your body frame and plenty of fine-tuning straps).
• A price range of $200 to $500.

Buying a pack online can be tough. It's better to go to an outdoor sports shop and pick the brains of the experts that work there. On site, you'll also have the chance to try out different packs, assessing their adjustability, weight distribution, and comfort.

New Twists on Backcountry Basics

• Compass Watch
These two essentials have been combined for easy access.
www.campmor.com

• Backcountry Gourmet
So long, aluminum foil-packaged cuisine. Hello, MaryJane's EcoPouch options: easy, organic, delicious!
www.maryjanesoutpost.org

• Klean Kanteen
Eco-friendly, reusable stainless steel water bottles. www.kleankanteen.com

• Headlamp
How many times have you tried to hold a flashlight in your teeth while rooting around in a dark tent to find something? A headlamp can free up your hands while you find your way. New "hybrid" headlamps have both LED and Xenon bulbs for bright, long-lasting illumination at long and short range. They're lightweight and compact, but tough enough to stand up to rigorous outdoor use. Black Diamond offers a large selection at www.bdel.com.

• ShillyShally
My own little creation, a ShillyShally is a bandanna with moxie. It's ready to become a bath towel, blankie, boa, you name it. Make one yourself from a three-foot-square piece of light cotton fabric, and gussy it up with a bit of embroidery or tie-dye. You'll be amazed how many uses (and how much comfort) you can wring out of a simple square of cloth!

• Outpost Jetboil
Jetboil is a "personal cooking system" that integrates cookware with camp stove in one compact little unit. The cookware is a one-liter insulated cooking cup with a removable cozy that reduces boil time and keeps your food warm longer. The cup has a lid with a pour spout that can double as a measuring cup, and a hard-anodized surface that is durable and easy to clean. The camp stove is a neat little combination of a "heat exchanger," "burner base," and a 3½-ounce fuel canister. The heat exchanger directs heat into your food, not into the air, and helps keep the wind out. The burner base attaches to the base of the cooking cup, and comes with a built-in piezoelectric igniter for matchless lighting. The fuel canister contains high-performance propane/isobutane fuel and can boil up to twelve liters of water, but is small enough to stow inside the cooking cup when not in use. www.jetboil.com

• Emergency Fire Starters
"Trick" birthday candles are small, easy to light, burn for several minutes, and will spontaneously relight in wind and rain. Dryer lint and steel wool make great easy-to-burn tinder, and either will stuff into a small pack pocket. Dry pine cones contain pitch, which burns nice and hot. Magnesium fire starters, available at outdoor equipment stores, use a small block of solid magnesium with a flint-sparking insert set into one edge.

A number of companies are cropping up that help you directly finance and increase market demand for renewable energy, sustainable land use projects, reduced waste, and travel practices that cut CO_2 emissions. Essentially, you invest in a healthier planet and you get credit for it to boot.

For more information, start with Sustainable Travel International (www.sustainabletravelinternational.org) and Native Energy (www.nativeenergy.com), both well-established companies that offer a number of investment options and solid guarantees as to how your dollars help wipe away your carbon footprint.

Sustainable Farming
I can't say enough about my favorite farmers' cooperative, Organic Valley. They are the largest cooperative of organic farmers in our country and one of our nation's leading organic brands. Organized in 1988, today it represents 1,100 farmers in twenty-nine states and one Canadian province with close to 400 million dollars in sales. Its founding mission is to save family farms through organic farming. They produce more than two hundred organic foods, including organic milk, soy, cheese, butter, spreads, creams, eggs, produce and juice, which are sold in supermarkets, natural foods stores, and food cooperatives nationwide. The same farmers who produce for Organic Valley also produce a full range of delicious organic meat under the Organic Prairie Family of Farms label. For further information, call 1-888-444-MILK or visit www.organicvalley.coop, and the cooperative's farmers' website, www.farmers.coop. One of their founders stopped by to visit my farm one day and ended up staying all day to help us put up hay. Now, *that's* cooperation!

Nature's Jewels

Bring along a bit of cotton string and make jewelry from objects found along the trail or in the garden. Seeds, shells, flowers, twigs, and bones can be strung together to create necklaces, ankle bracelets, crowns, or pretties for decorating your pack.

Outback artist Pen Brady believes that a river stone with a hole through it brings good luck. Wear one as a talisman on your trek, and then return it to the earth when you leave. Visit Pen's online gallery at www.penbrady.com .

Find more projects in *Jewelry From Nature: 45 Great Projects Using Sticks & Stones, Seeds & Bones* by Cathy Yow, and in my first book, *MaryJane's Ideabook, Cookbook, Lifebook—For the Farmgirl in All of Us*.

• **Backcountry Barter**

Looking to buy or sell outdoor gear? Post and search listings at MaryJane's Outpost (www.maryjanesoutpost.org).

Clean but Green

In the wild, it's critical to maintain good hygiene for your health, but not at the expense of the environment. Leave the scented soaps at home, and stick with more eco-friendly solutions.

Tips:

• Hot water and a washcloth can clean almost anything.
• Scrub away stubborn grime with wet sand, pebbles, or pine needles.
• Bring a spray bottle of plain old white vinegar to kill germs and rinse hair.
• If you forget your all-natural toothpaste, use a pinch of baking soda or mash wild strawberries into a tooth-cleaning paste.
• Use biodegradable soap sparingly, if at all. Because it is a chemical that requires soil to break down properly over time, make sure you keep it two hundred feet away (about seventy normal steps) from natural water sources.

Backcountry Bathroom

With your backpacker trowel, dig a "cat hole" six inches deep and at least two hundred feet from water sources. Squat above it and go. After wiping, place your toilet paper in the hole, fill in tightly with the soil you removed, and scatter with leaves. If you're in an area where you must pack out toilet paper, seal it in a plastic bag. Rocks, large leaves, snow, and moss can replace toilet paper in a pinch, but bury them too. Always follow with a vinegar hand spritz.

When packing for your period, consider using a DivaCup (www.divacup.com). It's an internal menstrual cup made of soft medical-grade silicone that is hypoallergenic and odorless. Because it's non-absorbent, it doesn't disrupt the natural vaginal environment or support bacterial growth. It only needs to be emptied two to four times a day and can be worn up to twelve hours overnight. Simply empty it in a cat hole, rinse with a spritz of vinegar and clean water, and pop it back into place. Remember to wash your hands before inserting and removing the cup. Pack out menstrual pads and tampons.

" *To be refreshed* by a morning walk
or an evening saunter ...
to be thrilled by the stars at night;
to be elated over a bird's nest or a
wildflower in spring—these are
some of the rewards of the simple life. "

– John Burroughs

MaryJane and Meg, 1982

"
Dear Momma,
Do you remember when Shalee and I went camping alone on the ridge? We were probably seven or eight. You helped us pack our sleeping bags, flashlights, and snacks so we could hike the two miles straight up. We spent the night, but I think we were mostly awake listening to all the little noises that go bump in the dark. I still remember barely being able to breathe when a pinecone fell from its tree near our sleeping bags. But just like you promised, watching the sunrise was an amazing reward for us two little girls, out there, all by our lonesome. We arrived home with our flashlight batteries completely dead. "

Love, Meg

Backpacking with kids is a different experience from going it alone or traveling with other adults. For me, the biggest challenge was adjusting my own expectations to accommodate a little person. Granted, I packed my daughter Meggie fifty-four miles through the Selway-Bitterroot Wilderness when she was just a sprout, but it wasn't the same as hiking that long stretch solo. The quiet intensity of trekking up the trail at my own pace, listening to the rhythm of my breath in time with my boots, was punctuated with stops, sidetracks, and inevitable squalls.

In the years that followed, Meggie and my son, Emil, both grew into capable wilderness kids who were eager to charge out and explore, but I soon realized that stops, sidetracks, and squalls were always going to be a part of family backpacking. I wasn't a lone young wilderness ranger anymore, I was a mom—and I learned to embrace the joys along with the challenges. Every rest stop became an opportunity to study the patterns of multi-colored lichen on a boulder. Every "I'm thirsty!" reminded me that I, too, could benefit from another cool drink of water. And each time I heard, "Momma, what's that?" I was reminded that there is no sweeter occupation in life than pausing for a moment to wonder.

In exchange for solitude and get-to-the-goal fervor, backpacking with babes provides precious opportunities for bonding, teaching, and enjoying our children. Together, you can escape to places beyond the din of society, where nature offers endless curiosities to explore. Maybe best of all, living out of a pack in the wild means relying on each other in more profound, instinctual ways than you're likely to encounter in normal everyday life, and it requires teamwork twenty-four hours a day—come hail or high water. Without a doubt, backcountry bonding can be a struggle, but there's nothing like trials by trail to create lifelong memories and true family ties.

Backpacks for Kids

According to the kid-gear experts at Upside Over, "The most important thing to consider when picking out a backpack is the 'torso fit range' or size. To find the torso length, measure your child's back along the spine from the top of their hip bones up to the C7 vertebrae, the knobby bone at the base of their neck."

When it comes to carrying capacity, the general rule is that kids should tote no more than one quarter of their bodyweight. Toddlers and young children (up to about eight years old), should shoulder less so that they don't over-exert and burn out before you've rounded the first bend. If your kids are anything like mine were, though, they'll beg to carry some kind of pack—it makes them feel grown-up and helpful. A fun idea these days is to equip your pint-sized packer with a hydration pack. The smallest versions hold about thirty-five ounces of water that a child can access through an attached straw-like tube whenever she needs it. Larger models carry water and a bit of light cargo as well. CamelBak and Kelty brands both offer hydration packs in children's sizes.

Your preteen can be expected to carry up to about twenty-two pounds (the actual weight limit will depend on the individual kid). Make sure she's having fun and not straining too much. Start off light and add more as she builds up strength and stamina.

Before embarking on an extended backpacking trip, it's always a good idea to warm-up with a few shorter trips to familiarize your child with wearing a pack and gauge her endurance. Be ready to carry your child's load in addition to your own should she decide it's too cumbersome. Better to keep her comfortable and happy than to spoil her enthusiasm with the impression that backpacking is backbreaking.

Upside Over (www.upsideover.com), REI (www.rei.com), and Campmor (www.campmor.com) offer a variety of backpacks for kids.

Hiking Pace

Because Mom or Dad will be packing baby in a kid carrier, you can set a pace that suits you. Just be prepared to stop and check baby frequently.

Toddlers can walk, and often demand to, but they tend to tucker out quickly. Give them a chance to feel out the trail with their own two feet, but don't rush. Wander with your toddler, watching out for obstacles and allowing time for joyful distractions (again, it's all about mind-set!). When she gets tired, put her in the kid pack and hit the trail.

Realistically, you can probably hike no more than about two to four miles per day, considering stops and slow periods. You might be able to manage more with older school-age children or if you're carrying your infant on your back. If your family can handle more, that's great! Just make sure everybody is happy and that you're allowing plenty of time for meals and rest breaks. The most important goal of family backpacking is to have fun.

Here's an idea for your week of quiet. How about trying your hand at basketry? A pine-needle basket specifically. Since finding a few pine needles isn't a problem in most outdoor areas, don't miss an opportunity to benefit from this form of serious "therapy." For inspiration or to buy a handmade basket, check out Idaho City's Lisa Marie Martinez, www.freewebs.com/lisamariesbasketry, before you go. A self-taught pine-needle weaver, her style is unique—often she incorporates gourds into her vessels and only uses needles from fallen trees. Her baskets are simply exquisite. All four featured here are Lisa Marie's.

7-day
BACKPACKING
Meal Plan
High Protein, No Fuss, Low Budget

If you were writing a screenplay about your life, you'd want to include the week you spent "out there" camping in that one perfect place—the place where you took the time to fill up your autobiographical bank simply because you could, because you weren't wearing a watch. You had the time to think about who you were, really. You'd describe your week with phrases like, "Clearly, something happened to me out there."

It was the week you connected with Mother Nature by eating the mother of all grains: quinoa—the grain with mystically ancient origins fed to Inca warriors, increasing their stamina and sharpening their ability to reason; the vital, gluten-free grain that almost became extinct. Your description of yourself that week might be similar to quinoa itself: somewhat nutty, slightly hard but tender, and sweet on the inside. You, too, felt rediscovered.

Known as "the gold of the Incas," quinoa (pronounced *keen-wa*) contains more complete protein than any other grain. Some varieties are more than 20 percent protein. Super easy to digest, it's light on the stomach (a natural for children or anyone needing a gluten-free diet). Unlike pastas or other grains, it's never sticky or heavy. A relative of spinach and Swiss chard, quinoa's seeds are quick and simple to prepare and high in essential trace minerals. Some predict it will be the "super-grain of the future" because of its unique qualities and flavor. I think it is unequivocally "the perfect food."

1 Easy Recipe, 21 unique meals . . .

But quinoa for seven days in a row? Yup, trust me on this one. It's not all that unusual to eat one type of grain as a basis for all your meals. If you stop to think about it, you've probably eaten wheat every day for at least seven days in a row before, if not for twenty-one! With my seven-day meal plan, you'll be adding other

Red Quinoa

White Quinoa

173

Since a cutting surface is hard to come by "out there," carrot "shavings" are a good way to practice your whittling skills.

fresh foods, nuts and fruits, cheeses, and a wide variety of distinct flavor blends, along with some edible wild greens. Remember, quinoa is easier to digest and has more protein than any other grain. It's lighter to pack and cooks quickly and easily without burning. You could substitute oats for the breakfast meals and millet or rice for some of the lunch and dinner meals I propose, but I'd hate you to miss out on how great this plan feels, how cleansing, how filling, and how simple it is. In fact, if you're ever feeling down and low on energy but your schedule won't allow you to get away "out there" to recharge, think of my seven-day eating plan as a good detoxification diet for recharging your batteries and giving you a fresh start.

Here's the other benefit to leaving home with a simplified meal plan in your backpack. When I'm "out there," what I need most are meals that are wholesome but predictable, easy, and routine. I don't want the fake energy that sugary snacks provide. I don't want the heavy protein that meat provides. I don't want any unexpected tummy upsets triggered by foods that are too rich or too salty. And I don't want to spend too much time getting ready before I go.

Let it go! You'll be just fine without taking along this and that and everything in between. Elaborate meal planning and fussing and fretting can sour you on taking future trips. Anyone who's a serious backpacker will tell you that fussing with food before the trip and then again during the outing gets old real quick. And you can always hope to supplement your meals with some fresh fish that you caught yourself (see page 137).

Having spent entire summers alone and "out there," I can say emphatically: I don't want any surprises (my normal life already has too many). I crave simplicity (the reason I wanted to get away from it all in the first place). I want time to think and decompress, meaning I want to embark on my week knowing that food won't use up too much of my "I'm finally free!" time.

Here's a little story to shore up my point about simplicity. Ten years ago, during harvest (back when we were still cutting hundreds of acres of wheat), I decided I needed to head out alone for three days. My teenage kids were finally old enough to drive our grain trucks and we had a farmhand for the first time. I loaded up my backpack with an array of my own signature organic backpacking foods (www.maryjanesoutpost.org), a stove, some cheese and crackers, and some apples. When I got to the trailhead at Race

Creek on the Selway River, I had the uncontrollable urge to really leave it all behind. My plan had been to hike into Three Links Bridge about ten miles and visit a spot full of memories, then turn around and hike back out. Instead, I left all my food and my stove in my truck except for the cheese, crackers, and apples. I hiked in only two miles and spent the entire time camped under one tree that had an active osprey nest next to a white sand beach. I swam, I read. I was given the rare opportunity to study in detail a mama osprey and her fledglings. I slept and thought. I slept so soundly those two nights that some chipmunks chewed a hole in my straw hat. I came home deeply rested, more so than if I'd pushed myself to perform. It wouldn't have felt good to lay so low for three days and eat the entire time. I needed an experience more lean, more renewing.

FIRST (up to several weeks ahead)
Use my shopping list & equipment list to:
- track down the essentials, either online or in your local co-op or health food store
- find the perfect camp stove and cook gear
- prepare three breakfast flavor blends
- prepare seven lunch/dinner flavor blends
- prepare seven snack and/or topping blends

NEXT (just before you go)
Shop locally to:
- choose a variety of cheeses
- pick up some good-looking carrots, oranges, and apples

FINALLY (once you're on the trail)
Use my "wild edibles guide" to:
- forage for some greens or edible flowers

Lists, Recipes, & Wild Guide Ahead

The Shopping List

I've arranged this list in alphabetical order so you can scan it easily and cross off the items you already have on hand. If my list calls for only one teaspoon of something and you don't have it on hand, consider a shopping trip to a food co-op or health food store, where bulk herbs and spices are available in amounts as little as one teaspoon. Remember, you'll be making seven different blends for use in fourteen lunches and dinners. In other words, you'll use each one of my blends twice during the week you're "out there." The mix and match is up to you. There's a little bit extra of each blend in case you identify an absolute favorite and want to eat it more than twice during your week. So for the mix and match, let's say on Monday, you eat the Hawaiian blend for lunch. On Thursday night, you can eat it again, this time with a sprinkling of the dried cottage cheese-pineapple topping recipe on page 188. If you're like the others who've tried my plan, you'll have identified your favorite blends by the end of the week for back-home use in scrambled eggs, spaghetti and pizza sauces, stir-fry dishes, and more.

Organic
is always best

Organic and LOCAL
even better

ORGANIC HOMEGROWN
the very best!

Fruits, Dried

❖ www.shopnatural.com
Bananas, dried whole then sliced in 1/2-inch
   pieces, 1/2 lb
Blueberries, 1/2 lb
Cranberries, fruit-juice sweetened
Currants, 1/2 lb
Goji Berries, 1/2 lb
Raisins (Golden), 1/2 lb

Herbs, Spices, and Flavorings

❖ www.shopnatural.com
Allspice, 1/2 t
Basil, 3 T
Black Pepper, 4 t
Black Pepper, 2 t
Caraway (crushed), 1 t
Cayenne, 1/4 t
Celery Seed, 1 t
Cinnamon, 3 T
Citric Acid, 1/2 t
Coriander, 6 T
Cumin, 6 T
Curry Powder, 2 T
Garlic Powder, 6 T
Ginger, 3 T
Mint, 2 T
Mustard Powder, 1 t
Nutmeg, 1 t
Onion Flakes, 2 t
Oregano, 3 T
Parsley, 4 T
Paprika, 1 t
Pepper (Red, crushed), 2 1/2 t
Saffron, few threads
Salt, 1/4 c
Star Anise, 2 t
Thyme, 1 T
Turmeric, 2 t

"Milk" Powders and Shreds

❖ www.wildernessfamilynaturals.com
Coconut Milk Powder, 1 1/2 c
Coconut Shreds, 1/4 c

❖ www.organicvalley.coop
❖ www.shopnatural.com
Milk Powder, 1 1/2 c
Soymilk Powder, 1 1/2 c

Nuts

❖ www.wildernessfamilynaturals.com
Almonds, 1/2 lb
Cashews, 1/2 lb
Peanuts, 1 lb
Pecans, 1/2 lb
Walnuts, 1/2 lb

Seeds & Grains

❖ www.shopnatural.com
Flax Seed, 1 T
Sesame Seeds, 1/4 c
Sunflower Seeds, 1/2 lb
Quinoa, 7 lbs total (5 1/2 lbs white + 1 1/2 lbs red)
*Note: Quinoa has a natural coating called saponin that can
create a bitter taste. Earlier varieties required rinsing before
use. Pre-rinsed quinoa is now commonly available.

Sweeteners

❖ www.auntpattys.com
Honey (Dried), 3/4 c
Molasses (Dried), 1/2 c
Sucanat, 1/2 c + 4 t

Optional

Bonito (see page 185)
Sea Vegetables (see page 185)
Hemp Seed (see page 185)
Coffee/Tea
Brown Sugar
Butter

LAST-MINUTE SHOPPING LIST:

Just before you go, shop locally to pick up the following supplies:

Cheeses (hard): 3 lbs total (Try some exotic cheeses like Asiago, Parmesan, and Pecorino/Romano; or
Spanish sheep's-milk cheeses like Idiazabal and Manchego.)

Fresh Produce: 7 Apples, 7 Carrots, 7 Oranges

The Equipment List

You'll need a:
- Spoon
- Cup
- Bowl
- Pocket Knife
- Stove

LOOKING BACK ...

To better appreciate this story, you need to flip ahead to page 222, where I'm bent down drinking water, surrounded by large boulders. The mountain range where I worked as a wilderness ranger that summer had massive talus (a sloping mass of rocky fragments) at the base of Red Castle Mountain, all of it above timberline in the Uinta Mountains.

I spent my first summer there perfecting my ability to move fast, rock to rock, skittering along the tops of them like a mama lion, knowing that one false move and my foot might wedge between rocks too big to move. My personal obstacle course was thousands of acres. It's a lot like I imagine tightrope walking to be. The key to staying upright? Keep moving once you start! Don't look down. Go. The momentum itself seemed to provide sure feet, feet that touched down too briefly to find trouble. I wore out four pairs of boots "hopping to it" those two summers.

I'd been cleaning fish that day. Instead of immediately putting my knife back into my little handmade leather holster, I knocked it with my foot. The pocketknife my father gave me fell into the treacherous rocks in the water below, permanently gone.

The next season, with another knife on my belt, this time a different color, I was again fishing, patches of melting snow all around, when I spotted something red on a rock in the distance. There, on top of a boulder, sat my knife, one year later.

For cooking, the Jetboil is my stove of preference because the vessel in which you bring the water to a boil is insulated, meaning you use a lot less fuel. This makes cooking the quinoa a snap because you merely add the water and quinoa, bring it to a boil, turn the heat off, and put the lid on. (For coffee lovers, the Jetboil also comes with an optional coffee press.) Visit www.jetboil.com for retailers. If you already have another type of stove, see page 188 for my instructions on how to make a lightweight insulated "pot cozy."

For utensils, you can go with some high-tech backpacking ware made from lightweight materials like titanium. But I prefer old-fashioned enamelware. However, instead of a bowl, I prefer a small saucepan that I use for a bowl so that if I decide to cook over an open campfire, I also have a vessel for that purpose. Your cup can double as a measuring cup by marking measurement lines on it with a permanent marker.

Here's how you'll make up your daily batches of quinoa:

Each morning, you'll put 1 cup quinoa into your cookpot along with 2 cups water. You'll bring it to a boil, then turn the heat off and put the lid on. In 20–30 minutes, you'll have enough quinoa for your breakfast and lunch.

For your breakfast meals, you'll use 1 1/2 cups of the cooked quinoa, mix in a breakfast flavor blend, add apples or oranges, then add a topping blend. For your lunch meals, you'll use 1 1/2 cups of the cooked quinoa, then add a lunch/dinner flavor blend along with your choice of cheese and maybe some carrots or wild edibles.

Each evening as you're setting up camp, you'll put 1/2 cup quinoa into your cookpot along with 1 cup water. You'll bring it to a boil, then turn the heat off and put the lid on. In 20–30 minutes, you'll have your dinner quinoa ready for the addition of your flavor blend, topping blend, cheese, fresh produce, and/or wild edibles.

For a decadent dessert, make a batch of quinoa, then toss in a pat of butter, 1 T brown sugar, and an apple. (I'm a big fan of fresh-grated nutmeg, so I pack a miniature grater and a couple of egg-shaped nutmeg seeds.)

START WITH QUINOA

ADD A FLAVOR BLEND

ADD FRUIT

ADD A TOPPING BLEND

My flavor blends allow you to use quinoa as a base for experiencing close to two dozen different meals. They're also lightweight and compact and fit nicely into little travel baggies. The breakfast blends have some flexibility because someone like me who *loves* coconut milk can take only that blend; someone who is allergic to cow's milk can go with the soy blend instead. Experiment at home before you go. The following flavor blend recipes (breakfast, lunch, dinner, and snacks and toppings) make up more than you'll need for seven days. (See shopping list on page 177.)

Breakfast
FLAVOR BLENDS

> Add **4 tablespoons** Flavor Blend to
> **1 1/2 cups** cooked quinoa (1/2 lb uncooked).

Coconut Milk + Honey
(makes 2 cups)
Cinnamon, 1 t
Coconut Milk Powder, 1 1/4 c
Ginger, 1 t
Honey (Dried), 3/4 c

Milk + Sucanat
(makes 2 cups)
Cinnamon, 1 t
Milk Powder, 1 1/2 c
Nutmeg, 1/2 t
Sucanat, 1/2 c

Soymilk + Molasses
(makes 2 cups)
Cinnamon, 2 t
Flax Seed, 1 T
Molasses (Dried), 1/2 c
Soymilk Powder, 1 1/2 c

"All happiness depends on a leisurely breakfast."
– John Gunther

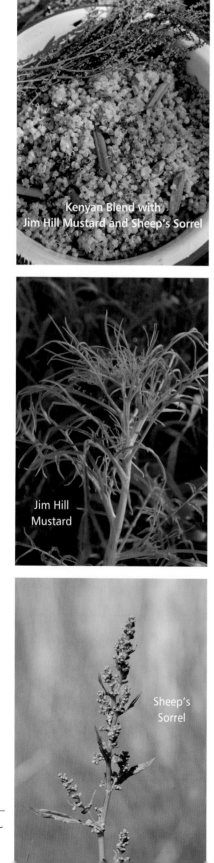

Kenyan Blend with
Jim Hill Mustard and Sheep's Sorrel

Jim Hill
Mustard

Sheep's
Sorrel

Lunch/Dinner
FLAVOR BLENDS

Add **2 teaspoons** Flavor Blend to
1 1/2 cups cooked quinoa (1/2 lb. uncooked).

Part of my entertainment when I'm "out there" in the wild is the pursuit of wild edibles (see the "Wild Edibles Guide" starting on page 190). Even as a child, I was always putting little bits of this and that into my food, but the first wild salad I harvested and ate was a bowl of "spring beauties," roots and all, washed off in a high-altitude lake. Similar to radishes in flavor, that bowl of tiny white flowers, reddish-hued and pink-veined, probably took an hour to gather. But like poet William Blake said, "to see … heaven in a wildflower, hold infinity in the palm of your hand," it's even better to taste heaven in a bowl. That salad, the result of stalking down and foraging high and low the most beautiful of wild flowers, was entertainment at its very best. Wild edibles like the common Jim Hill Mustard, Sheep's Sorrel, and Lamb's Quarters pictured here not only add important decorum to your "out there" time, they add essential nutrients to your dried meals.

Kenyan Blend (makes 1/2 cup)

Caraway (crushed), 1 t
Cayenne, 1/8 t
Coriander, 1 T + 1 t
Cumin, 1 T

Mint, 2 T
Saffron, few threads
Salt, 1 t

OUTSPOKEN...

Baroness Karen von Blixen-Finecke, 1885–1962 (pen name, Isak Dinesen), was a Danish author and Kenyan farmer best known for her memoir *Out of Africa*. About life at her African outpost, she said, "Here at long last one was in a position not to give a damn for all conventions; here was a new kind of freedom which until then one had only found in dreams!"

Santa Fe Blend (makes 1/2 cup)

Coriander, 1 T + 2 t
Cumin, 3 T
Garlic powder, 1 T
Oregano, 2 t

Paprika, 1 t
Red pepper flakes, 1 t
Salt, 1 t

OUTSPOKEN...

Dolores Huerta, 1930– , a labor organizer, social activist, and mother of eleven, co-founded the United Farm Workers with Cesar Chavez, bringing human rights to farm workers across the U.S. In 1988, while demonstrating peacefully against the policies of candidate George Bush, she was severely injured when police clubbed the demonstrators. She eventually won a considerable financial settlement, as well as changes in police policy on demonstrations. She's the recipient of numerous awards, including *Ms. Magazine*'s "Woman of the Year," *Ladies Home Journal*'s "100 Most Important Women of the 20th Century," and the Eleanor Roosevelt Human Rights Award.

Santa Fe Blend with Lamb's Quarters

Lamb's Quarters

Greek Blend (makes 1/2 cup)

Basil, 1 T
Black pepper, 2 t
Citric acid, 1/2 t
Garlic powder, 1 T + 1 t

Mustard powder, 1 t
Parsley, 4 T
Thyme, 1 T
Salt, 1 t

OUTSPOKEN...

Demeter is the Greek goddess of grain and the harvest. She taught mankind about agriculture, and she is also responsible for the seasons. When her daughter Persephone was abducted by Hades and taken to the underworld, Demeter wandered the earth in search of her lost child. During this time, the earth brought forth no grain. Eventually Persephone's father, Zeus, intervened and arranged her return. But Hades gave Persephone a pomegranate. When she ate from it, she was forever bound to spend a third of each year with him in the underworld, at which time winter returns to the earth.

Greek Blend with Carrots

Puerto Rican Blend with Sunflower Seeds, Raisins, and Wild Roses

Puerto Rican Blend (makes 1/2 cup)

Allspice, 1/2 t	Nutmeg, 1/2 t
Cinnamon, 1 t	Oregano, 2 T
Coconut Shreds, 1/4 c	Pepper (Red, crushed), 1 t
Garlic Powder, 1 t	Salt, 1 t
Ginger, 1 t	

OUTSPOKEN...

Rita Moreno, 1931– , is a singer, dancer, and actress, and the first and only Puerto Rican actress in history (as well as one of only nine people) to have won an Emmy, a Grammy, an Oscar, and a Tony Award. She's perhaps best known for her role as the feisty Anita in the film version of *West Side Story*. Of her success, she says, "I never stopped aspiring."

Wild Roses

Curry Blend (makes 1/2 cup)

Black Pepper, 2 t	Cumin, 1 T + 1 t
Cayenne, pinch	Curry Powder, 1 T + 1 t
Cinnamon, 2 t	Turmeric, 2 t
Coriander, 2 T + 2 t	Salt, 1 T + 1 t

OUTSPOKEN...

Arundhati Roy, 1961– , is an Indian novelist, writer, and activist. In 2002, she won the Lannan Foundation's Cultural Freedom Award for "her ongoing work in the struggle for freedom, justice, and cultural diversity." She was also awarded the Sydney Peace Prize in 2004. She says, "Another world is not only possible, she is on her way. On a quiet day, I can hear her breathing."

Curry Blend with Miner's Lettuce and Cheese

Miner's Lettuce

Bejing Blend (makes 1/2 cup)

Black Pepper, 2 t
Celery Seed, 1 t
Cinnamon, 2 t
Ginger, 1 T

Onion Flakes, 2 t
Salt, 2 t
Sesame Seeds, 1/4 c
Star Anise, 2 t

OUTSPOKEN...

Polly Bemis, 1853–1933, was born Lalu Nathoy near Bejing, China, to impoverished farmers, sold to bandits during a drought for two bags of seed, shipped to America, and auctioned off as a slave to a mining camp owner in Warren, Idaho. She worked there until she won her freedom, then ran a boarding house, married the local saloon keeper (after Idaho modified its law against mixed-race unions), and became the foremost pioneer of the remote Salmon River area. Her life story was fictionalized in the book and movie, *A Thousand Pieces of Gold.*

Hawaiian Blend (makes 1/2 cup)

Basil, 2 T
Coconut Milk Powder, 4 T
Garlic Powder, 2 T

Ginger, 1 t
Pepper (Red, crushed), 1/2 t
Sucanat, 4 t

OUTSPOKEN...

Queen Lydia Lili'uokalani, 1838–1917, was the last reigning monarch of the Hawaiian islands. She worked to frame a new constitution that would restore power to native Hawaiians to replace one previously signed under threat of force. Her government was overthrown by the U.S. in 1893, but when President Grover Cleveland concluded that the overthrow was illegal and offered to give back the throne if the Queen granted amnesty to everyone responsible, she refused on principle. She later rescinded, but eventually Lili'uokalani lost her throne and the Hawaiian people lost their kingdom to U.S. sugar interests. She was also an accomplished author and songwriter. One of her best-known musical compositions is the song "Aloha 'Oe," which she wrote while confined for a year during her overthrow.

Hawaiian Blend with Bonito

For extra protein, add some dried super-lightweight bonito flakes to any of the dishes. Bonito, a type of mackerel, is steamed and dried, then shaved into flakes. It rehydrates in an instant. www.edenfoods.com

For extra minerals and flavor, add lightweight dried sea vegetables like hiziki to any of the dishes. It easily rehydrates in water. The black, tiny, tight curls are hand harvested in the wild from the environmentally protected waters of Ise (ee-say), Japan, then washed, steamed, and dried. It expands to about four times its size when rehydrated for 10 minutes in cold water. The flavor is mild but wonderfully salty. www.edenfoods.com

For a delicious dose of Omega 3 & 6 Essential Fatty Acids (EFAs), add some shelled hemp seed to any of the dishes, especially the breakfast dishes. This brand of hemp seed has the hull removed, exposing the soft and creamy "butter" inside. www.manitobaharvest.com

Snack & Topping
BLENDS

> Mix **1/2 lb** dried fruit and
> **1/2 lb** nuts or seeds.

I don't blend my fruits and nuts into one big bag of mix because I want to look forward to something new and different every day. If you're changing what you nibble on, you're less likely to develop an allergy to any one seed or nut. Trail mixes that have sugary sweets make it hard to keep your energy levels consistent throughout the day—a must when you're hiking. You need steady and strong, not spike then spent. These are my favorite sugar-free combinations.

Pecans & Cranberries (orange-juice sweetened)

Peanuts & Bananas

Almonds & Goji Berries

Sunflower Seeds
& Currants

Walnuts
& Raisins

Peanuts
& Blueberries

Cashews
& Cranberries
(apple-juice
sweetened)

Drying Cottage Cheese

This combination never gets old when you're on the trail. Twenty years ago, I used to create this concoction by buying both ingredients freeze-dried in gallon cans, but home-dried is even better!

14   oz crushed pineapple, drained
16   oz cottage cheese, drained

Combine ingredients and puree in food processor. Spread on square sheet of Teflon (www.dryit.com) and place on a screen in the dehydrator, leaving a one-inch border between Teflon and the edge. Dry on medium overnight (time may vary with different dehydrators).

Make a Quinoa Pot Cozy

If you don't have a Jetboil (the stove I recommend for my "7-day Backpacking Meal Plan," page 178), but you DO have another type of cannister stove that will heat water, here's a pot cozy you can make at home. Using a pot cozy will save you fuel and will also ensure perfectly cooked quinoa every time. Follow the instructions on page 179, remove your pot from the heat, and "tuck" the pot into your pot cozy for 15 minutes or until quinoa is ready.

Ever get those shiny bright, glossy, wasteful-looking mailers along with your samples of whatever? Well, you can recycle them into a pot cozy. I've used my recycled pot cozy for five years! You still have to buy the heat tape and splice the layers together (so you have double-sided aluminum—the mailers usually have clear plastic on the inside), but recycle them you can. If you're not worried about the weight, some good old-fashioned duct tape will work.

Materials and Tools:
Reflectix Insulation
   (2' length for a small pot or 3' length for a large pot)
Heat Tape or Metal Repair Tape
Scissors
Yardstick
Measuring Tape
Permanent Marker

Instructions:

1. Place your pot onto the Reflectix insulation rim down. Trace around rim. This will serve as the bottom of your cozy. Next, put the lid, rim down, on Reflectix insulation and trace. This will be the top. Cut out both top and bottom pieces. If your lid has a handle, set the top piece on pot lid to determine lid handle placement. Mark and then cut a small hole. Insert handle in hole. Set lid and insulated cover aside.

2. Measure around the circumference of your pot; add 1 1/4" to the total. Next, measure the height of your pot, including lid; add 1 1/4" to the total. Using your yardstick, draw a rectangle with the final height and circumference measurements onto the sheet of Reflectix. Cut out. Place a strip of tape of equal length along one of the Reflectix rough edges, so that half of the width of the tape is adhered to it and the other half remains free. This will be where you will attach the bottom of your cozy.

3. To attach the cozy bottom, place the pot on its side at one end of the Reflectix strip, so that the exposed side of the tape is facing you and the bottom of the pot just aligns with the edge of the Reflectix. Put the insulated bottom on the pot and hold it there. Then slowly roll your pot and its insulated bottom along the strip of Reflectix, making sure that the insulated bottom is being rolled along the tape and that it is adhering. Once the pot has been rolled all the way around the strip, fold the still exposed tape over the bottom insulation and smooth the tape edges. Now the bottom should be completely attached to the sides. Remove pot and reinsert to check its fit.

4. With the pot in the cozy, cut off the excess Reflectix so that the sides meet but do not overlap and the upper rim has an overhang of 1/2". Cut a notch for the pot handle if needed, tape side seam together, and place tape over any rough edges.

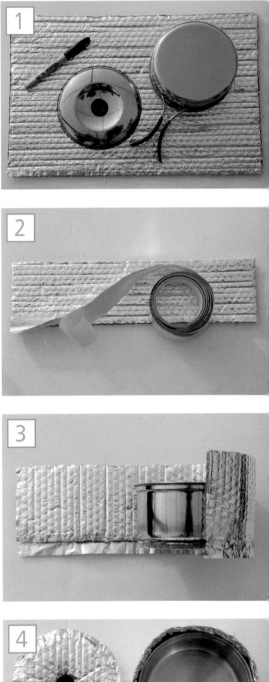

" *Wilderness* is not a luxury but a necessity of the human spirit. "

– Edward Abbey

Miner's lettuce *(Claytonia perfoliata)* makes a delicious and easy salad. Once you identify this little "free lettuce" gem, you'll find it hard to imagine how you could have missed it before. The stem bearing its cluster of tiny, white-to-pinkish flowers grows up through the middle of what appears to be a large, circular leaf (actually two leaves growing together). Add damsel's rocket flowers (page 208), dress, and enjoy!

Wild Edibles Guide

Getting Your Greens on the (Wild) Side

By the time spring finally starts to unfurl, we are not only craving sunshine and fresh air, we hanker for green. Green shoots, sprigs, and leaves tickle some instinct buried deep in our bellies and urge us to graze.

Whether you're an urban, suburban, or rural dweller, food for the taking is right outside your door. Sure, modern transportation may afford us the luxury of produce year-round, but there are undeniable benefits to eating food when it's in season. Fresh green goodies plucked straight from the earth are packed with vitamins, minerals, and disease-fighting phytochemicals that are compromised when plants are harvested before they're ripe, then stored and shipped to far-off places. You don't even need to garden in order to enjoy the luxury of seasonal greens. Scores of familiar wild plants (many are known as "weeds") can provide interesting and nutritious additions to your diet. Plus, fresh-picked wild greens you've harvested yourself taste better, plain and simple—and they're free! Not to mention, foraging is an outdoor activity that completely sucks you in—recreation with a purpose.

All you need is a bit of knowledge about what's safe to eat and what's not, and you're on your way to sensational salads and more. Some cities are even beginning to offer guided foraging tours in their parks. Remember to forage in clean, uncontaminated areas at least fifty feet away from heavy traffic and avoid heavily sprayed areas such as railroad right-of-ways. Once you learn how to recognize the cornucopia of wild edibles within your reach, foraging for food will improve your meals *and* your health.

There are hundreds of edible wild plants out there, and many are specific to certain regions or climate zones. I've gathered up eight wild greens commonly found throughout the United States that are easy to recognize, safe to eat, healthy, and downright delicious. I've even included a selection of recipes that'll inspire you to start exploring nature's gifts.

Watch out

for poisonous wild plants! Whenever you set out in search of wild greens, be sure you can positively identify what you're picking. Some poisonous plants resemble edible spring greens. Consult a field guide or contact a natural resource professional if you're unsure about any plant.

Salad Spoon Revisited

In my first book, *MaryJane's Ideabook, Cookbook, Lifebook—For the Farmgirl in All of Us*, I elaborated on my concept of eating salad with a spoon. I got so many letters and such positive feedback from readers, I thought it was worth revisiting. Wash and cut the stems off your gathered and/or garden treasures, and put everything on a large cutting board. Chop until the wondrous parts are quite small and fit for a spoon. You'll be eating three to four times more greens this way. And, with a spoon, your children will eat more salad too, fueling their bodies with critical nutrients.

If you do not have access to the wild edible greens listed in these recipes, you may substitute other domestic greens. Though some wild edibles have stronger, or "earthier" flavors, so do a lot of domestic greens. Some of the substitutions I like are: romaine for purslane, spinach for lambsquarters, Swiss chard (remove the ribs) for wintercress and watercress, arugula for dandelion greens, tat soi for chickweed.

Lambsquarters

Chenopodium album

Description

Lambsquarters, also called goosefoot, is a relative of spinach and beets. The plant branches like a tree, reaching 3 to 5 (sometimes up to 10) feet tall. Its diamond-shaped leaves have jagged edges, grow up to four inches long, and look like they've been dusted with white powder underneath. The tiny greenish flowers that hang from the upper branches in spire-like clusters in summer can also be eaten.

Health Benefits

Lambsquarters boasts more beta-carotene, calcium, potassium, and iron than spinach, and is also an excellent source of vitamins C and B.

Harvesting

The best time to harvest lambsquarters is mid-spring to summer when the plant is only a few inches high. Gather the young shoots with leaves. The uppermost (youngest) leaves can also be used even when the plant has grown several feet high (summer to fall).

Preparation

To prepare, wash leaves and shoots thoroughly. Use as a spinach substitute in dishes like salad, soup, quiche, and veggie lasagna.

Lambsquarters and Lentil Stew (6 servings)

1/2	c onion, chopped
1/2	c celery, chopped
1/2	c carrots, chopped
1	T olive oil
2	t thyme
1/2	c tomato sauce
7 1/2	c vegetable or chicken stock
1 1/2	c lentils, sorted, washed, and drained
3	c lambsquarters
1/2	t salt (depending on saltiness of stock)

Fresh-cracked pepper

1	T sherry vinegar

In a stock pot, sauté the onion, celery, and carrots in olive oil until softened. Add 1 t thyme, tomato sauce, stock, and lentils. Bring to a boil, then reduce heat and simmer until lentils are almost tender, about 30 minutes. Add the lambsquarters, salt, pepper, the rest of the thyme, and vinegar. Continue to simmer for about 15 minutes, until the lentils are soft.

Purslane
Portulaca oleracea

Description
Purslane grows flat along the ground with rubbery reddish-green stems branching in every direction. The thick, fleshy leaves are oval shaped and grow close to the stem (no leaf stalks). Tiny bright yellow flowers bloom only in late summer and fall in the morning sunshine.

Health Benefits
Purslane is a terrific plant source of omega-3 fatty acids and iron. It is also high in vitamin C and contains beta-carotene and calcium.

Harvesting
Purslane grows from late spring to fall on sunny ground that has been disturbed, like an area that has been tilled for a garden, but can also be found growing in partial shade. The entire plant is edible, but if only the leafy tips are gathered, the plant will continue to grow and replace the tips for picking again. Safety tip: snap a stem, and if there's white milky sap inside, it could be a poisonous plant that resembles purslane—DON'T eat it. Purslane stems have clear, watery liquid inside like an aloe vera plant.

Preparation
Purslane can be washed, eaten raw or cooked, and served just like spinach. The leaves and sweet-and-sour stems make tasty salad greens. Chopped purslane can be used as a thickening agent in soups, it's delicious sautéed in butter, and the thick stems make excellent mini-pickles.

Indian Cucumber and Purslane Salad
(4 servings)

4	medium cucumbers, peeled, seeded, and chopped into 3/4-inch pieces
2	c purslane, leaves only
1/4	c finely chopped cilantro
1/4	c finely chopped onion
1	t cumin seeds, toasted
2	T vegetable oil (I prefer sunflower oil)
2	T rice vinegar
1/2	t salt

Place the cucumbers, purslane, cilantro, and onion in a bowl. Toast the cumin seeds in a small, hot saucepan until fragrant, about 1 minute. Combine seeds with the oil, vinegar, and salt. Toss with the vegetables and serve.

195

"A *weed* is only a plant whose virtues have not yet been discovered."

– Ralph Waldo Emerson

Chickweed
Stellaria media

Description
Chickweed is a delicate plant that either trails on the ground or forms mats 3 to 8 inches tall. The leaves are smooth-edged and spade-shaped, 1/2 to 1 inch long, and grow in pairs along a slender stem with one thin line of hairs along it, like a median strip down a highway. The tiny flowers have 5 white petals (though they're split, so they look like 10).

Health Benefits
Chickweed is full of vitamins B6, B12, C and D, plus beta-carotene, iron, calcium, potassium, zinc, phosphorus and manganese. Herbal nutritionists prescribe chickweed tea as a diuretic to cleanse the urinary tract.

Harvesting
Chickweed grows in sunny areas, as well as in partial shade. It is most abundant and flavorful in early spring, but can actually be harvested year round. Although new growth is the most desirable, the more "stem-y" old growth can be used when finely chopped.

Preparation
Chickweed tastes like fresh corn when raw and somewhat like spinach when steamed, simmered, or sautéed. For tea, steep 1 to 2 T of fresh chickweed in 1 c boiling water for 20 minutes.

Greek Chickweed Salad (4 servings)
2	c tender chickweed greens
3	c romaine lettuce, chopped
1/2	c crumbled feta cheese
1	cucumber, quartered lengthwise and chopped
1	tomato, chopped
1	garlic clove, minced
2	T lemon juice

Pinch of salt, pepper, and oregano

3	T olive oil

Chop greens and toss with the feta, cucumber, and tomato. Combine garlic, lemon juice, and spices in a food processor or bowl. Add oil in a slow stream, whisking vigorously. Toss dressing with salad and serve immediately.

Chickweed Pesto
(approx. 2 cups)
2	c chickweed greens
3	T walnut pieces
2	cloves garlic, minced
1/4	t salt
1	T lemon juice
1/2	c Parmesan cheese, grated
1/2	c olive oil, extra virgin

Add greens to a blender or food processor; pulse. Add remaining ingredients, saving the olive oil for last. Add the oil slowly in a stream until incorporated.

Watercress
Nasturtium officinale

Description

Vibrant green watercress grows in the cold, gentle waters of springs and creeks. Its smooth compound leaves have lots of round 1-inch wide leaflets. The leaves and stems are partially submerged during growth.

Health Benefits

Watercress is full of nutrients and can be harvested just after winter's thaw, making it a revitalizing spring tonic. It's a good source of vitamins A and C, along with niacin, thiamine, riboflavin, and iron.

Harvesting

According to folklore, watercress is edible any month that has an "R" in it, so the period of May through August is considered the off-season (leaves become rank in flavor when flower buds appear). Harvest handfuls of leaves here and there, thinning in patches but leaving some to continue growing.

Preparation

Wash leaves thoroughly with clean water, and place them in plastic bags to keep in the refrigerator crisper until used. Periodic sprinkling helps keep them fresh for about a week. Watercress has a hot, spicy taste, kind of like radishes. The pungent leaves and young stems are widely used for garnishing and in salads. When cooked or dehydrated, they release a flowery aroma, almost like vanilla. Try it raw in pesto or hot in sauces or stir-fries.

Shrimp and Watercress Salad (4 servings)

1 lb shrimp, large, peeled and deveined
1 small red onion, sliced very thinly
1 red grapefruit or blood orange
2 navel oranges
1 T mint leaves, chopped
2 c watercress, loosely packed

Vinaigrette:

3 T grapefruit juice
2 T sunflower oil
1 T red wine vinegar
1 t sugar
1/2 t salt
Fresh cracked pepper

To cook shrimp, bring a pot of water to a boil, add the shrimp, and remove the pot from heat. The shrimp will cook in 6 minutes or less. Remove shrimp from the pot and place in fridge. Prepare vinaigrette, adding oil at the very end in a thin stream while whisking. Slice navel ends off of the fruit, removing peel and as much pith as possible. Separate into sections and slice orange sections in half and grapefruit sections into thirds. Toss some of the vinaigrette with watercress and arrange on a plate. Toss fruit with shrimp, onion, mint, and remainder of dressing. Spoon fruit mixture on top of watercress.

Makes four main-course salads

Soba Noodles with Miso and Watercress

(4 servings)

8 oz soba noodles
2 T miso paste
4 T tamari
3 T water
2 T rice vinegar
2 t fresh grated ginger
1 garlic clove, minced
2 c watercress, loosely packed (1 medium bunch, with tough stems removed)

Cook soba noodles according to directions on the package. Combine next seven ingredients through garlic and bring to a simmer and slightly thick. (Add more miso paste or water according to taste, as different types of miso are stronger than others.) Remove sauce from heat. Stir in watercress and immediately pour over hot soba noodles. Serve.

LOOKING BACK ...

Papa Butters was crazy in love with watercress. He religiously cultivated its wildness in our ditch for use in his favorite snack. In the mood for something peppery when he gardened, he'd grab a salt shaker and a single slice of Momma's homemade bread. He'd hold the slice cupped in the fold of his hand and then cram as much watercress into the "burrito" as he could. He'd sprinkle it with salt, then fold it shut and eat it. That was it. "Blessed with cress," he used to say.

Wintercress
Barbarea vulgaris

Description

Wintercress (also called garden yellowrocket and creecy greens) is a fast-growing plant that begins as a flat basal rosette and later grows an upright stalk about a foot and a half high. A sprig of wintercress has one to five pairs of small lateral leaves below a large, rounded end leaf.

Health Benefits

Yet another nickname for wintercress is "scurvy grass" due to its high concentration of vitamin C.

Harvesting

The most remarkable feature of wintercress is its availability during cold weather. In fact, its scientific name, *Barbarea vulgaris*, refers to St. Barbara's Day (December 4) because it can be harvested in winter. The leaves are generally harvested in early spring, and flower buds can later be picked like wild broccoli. Choose cress with dark green leaves and no sign of yellowing.

Preparation

The youngest leaves make a tangy-crisp raw salad green, and more mature blades can be boiled or steamed. In late spring, boil unopened flower buds for five minutes, just as you would broccoli.

Wintercress Quiche (8 servings)

Crust:
1 1/2 c plus 2 T all-purpose, unbleached flour
1/2   t salt
10   T unsalted butter, cold, cut into 1/2-inch cubes
3   T ice water

Filling:
1   medium onion, chopped
1   clove garlic, minced
1   T butter
2   c loosely packed wintercress greens, well washed
3   eggs plus two egg yolks, beaten
1   c grated cheese (like sharp white cheddar)
1 1/4 c whipping cream
1/2   t salt
Fresh cracked pepper

Prepare crust: Combine flour and salt; cut in butter until crumbly. Add ice water, stirring just until the dough comes together. Form into a four-inch disk, wrap in parchment and chill for at least 30 minutes. After chilling, roll out pastry on a lightly floured surface to 1/8 inch thick. Fold in half, fold in half again, transfer to glass pie dish, and unfold. Crimp the edges and prick with a fork. Line pastry with parchment paper and fill with dried beans or pie weights. Bake at 375°F for 12 minutes. Remove from oven, remove parchment and beans, and return to oven for five more minutes. Cool slightly.

For the filling, sauté the onion and garlic in butter. Add the greens and sauté just until wilted, about 1 minute, and remove from heat. Spread mixture on bottom of pie shell. Whisk eggs, cheese, cream, and seasonings and pour over vegetable mixture. Bake at 375° for 30–40 minutes until top is light golden brown and filling is set in the middle. Cool slightly before cutting and serve warm or at room temperature.

OUTSPOKEN...

Tiffany Reynolds had a crochet hook, yarn scraps, and a dream of making a difference. "I wanted answers for my life and I wanted to make a difference in the lives of other women," Tiffany, a single mom of five, explains. "As I looked at my résumé, I wasn't so sure. I'd spent fifteen years as a stay-home mom. But some of the most beautiful things come from pulling together the lessons we've learned from life's unraveled projects."

Tiffany began attending knitting circles, teaching crochet workshops, and creating a line of patterns with the intention of sharing a percent of sales with Women in Renewal, an organization offering shelter and education against domestic violence. The patterns are now being distributed through Muench Yarns in California, and several designs have also been published by Interweave Press.

With the help of friends, Tiffany is working to organize a "Hooks and Hiking Boots Off the Beaten Path" workshop retreat. "We thought it would be a great opportunity to share some of the things we love: hiking or snowshoeing to a remote cabin, having hot soup, crocheting by the fire. It's a really awesome, renewing experience for all involved."

Tiffany's vibrant hats, bags, rugs, patterns, and more are available at www.cumicrochet.com.

"I have to work fast when the dandelions bloom. I left them a little too long, and mine are all wishes now ..."

Dandelions
Taraxacum officinale

Description
Young leaves, 2 to 6 inches in length, form a basal rosette. They are oblong and sometimes sparsely hairy with lobes that point toward the center of the rosette. A cluster of bright yellow flowers (each yellow "petal" is actually an individual flower), about 1 1/2 inches in diameter sit on the end of unbranched, leafless, hollow stalks (scapes) that are 2 to 6 inches tall. Of all the wild greens, dandelions are the most commonly known, gathered, and eaten. They've been used for thousands of years, and now they're even being cultivated for sale in big city gourmet markets.

Health Benefits
Dandelions are rich in vitamins A, C, B6, riboflavin, thiamine, calcium, copper, manganese, and iron. They're also packed with protein, choline, inulin, and pectin.

Harvesting
Pick young, tender leaves in the spring before the flower stalk appears. Be sure to include the underground leaf crowns or "rosettes." The developing yellow flower buds can also be dug up before they sprout (you'll find them nestled in the white crowns). Dandelion leaves are more tender and less strong-tasting if they are deprived of sunlight first. This can be accomplished by putting a cardboard box over a patch of dandelions for a week or two before you harvest them.

Dandelion roots, which can reach up to a foot and a half in length, can be dug up in early spring or late fall. These are the best times to harvest since most of the plant's nutrients are being stored in the roots. Choose areas where the soil is soft for easier digging (undisturbed areas usually yield bigger roots than mowed lawns).

Preparation
• Boil dandelion greens until tender (change the water once to mellow their tangy taste), then garnish with butter or lemon juice.
• Water in which the greens are cooked can be saved and sipped as a spring tonic.
• Unsprouted yellow flower buds make excellent boiled vegetables.
• The energy-filled root can be prepared as a mini-parsnip, or roasted to make dandelion root coffee (see recipe at right).

Roasted Dandelion Root "Coffee"
When brewed properly, dandelion root coffee closely resembles the rich flavor of traditional coffee, and it contains a wealth of vitamins and minerals.

Gather:
One 5-gallon bucket of dandelion roots (to yield about 10 gallons of coffee).

Prepare the Roots
To wash the roots, fill the bucket with water and agitate the roots with your hands. Pour off the muddy water and repeat this process a few times till the water runs clear and you have a pile of luscious golden roots. Don't worry if there's still some dirt left on them—you'll wash them again after chopping. With a sturdy knife, cut the roots into chunks. Put these into a large bowl (or sink), fill with water, then rub the roots and rinse till clean. Drain till fairly dry or pat with a towel.

Chop about 2 cups of root chunks at a time in your food processor till they're chopped into small, coarse bits.

Roasting the Roots

Spread the coarsely ground roots on cookie sheets about 1/2-inch thick. Place as many sheets as you can fit into your oven, set at 250°F, and leave the oven door slightly ajar to let moisture escape. The roasting process takes about 2 hours. Stir frequently and rotate the cookie sheets occasionally to ensure even drying and roasting. As the roots dry, they'll shrink and darken to a rich coffee color—but be careful not to let them burn. Cool completely and store in glass jars. Flavorful additions such as anise, cinnamon, ginger, and carob can be added if you like.

Brewing the Coffee

You can either grind the roots in a coffee mill and brew in a coffee pot, or you can place the coarsely ground roots in a tea infuser and boil in a pot of water. Use 1 tablespoon of roasted roots for each cup of water (1/3 cup per quart of water). Adjust to your taste if you like it stronger or weaker. Add a dash of cream and sugar if you like, and enjoy a steaming cup of Roasted Dandelion Root Coffee!

" *Without my morning coffee,*
I'm just like a dried up piece of roast goat. "
– Johann Sebastian Bach

Dandy Greens Pasta (6 servings)

2   c dandelion greens, washed, drained, and stemmed
2   eggs
1   T olive oil
1/2   t salt
1 1/2 c flour

Combine dandy greens, oil, eggs, and salt in a blender until smooth. Transfer to a bowl. Gradually add flour, stirring with a wooden spoon until dough becomes incorporated. Turn dough out onto surface and knead for 2 minutes. Roll out 1/8-inch thick. Dry 1 hour on surface before cutting into long noodles or other shapes. Cook in boiling water for about 3 minutes.

Wilted Dandelion Greens Salad

(4 servings)

2   T olive oil
2   shallots, chopped
1   garlic clove, minced
2   T golden raisins
2   T red wine vinegar
1   lb fresh dandelion greens, washed and stemmed
3   slices cooked bacon
1   apple, cored and sliced into very thin pieces
Salt and freshly cracked pepper

Heat oil in a wide saucepan and sauté shallots for 1 minute over medium heat. Add garlic and cook for 30 seconds, until barely browned. Stir in the golden raisins and vinegar, cooking for a few minutes. Remove pan from heat and add the greens, tossing to wilt. Transfer to a large bowl and toss with bacon and sliced apple. Season with salt and pepper. Serve immediately.

Dandelion & Rose Petal Jelly

(approx. 4 four-ounce jars)

1	heaping c dandelion flowers (pulled from about two cups of gathered open flower clusters)
1	heaping c yellow rose petals (if you have no yellow roses, you can use all dandelion flowers; just double the amount)
2	c boiling water
2	scant T lemon juice (strained)
4	c sugar
3	oz liquid pectin
4	four-oz. canning jars and lids

Make sure you pick your dandelions well away from roadways or other chemically treated areas, and wash them before using. Pick the biggest, most fully-open flower clusters, as they are easier to pull the individual flowers from. Pluck the yellow flowers from the green parts. (You don't want the green parts, but it's hard to separate them, so don't stress if a few get in.) If you don't get enough dandelion flowers in one day of plucking, freeze the ones you have in a plastic container. You can keep plucking and freezing until you have enough for jelly-making day.

When you have enough flowers, make an infusion: pour 2 cups of boiling water over the flowers and let them steep for 24 hours. Cover and refrigerate overnight. The next day, strain the flowers out of the infusion—first through a fine sieve, and then through a paper coffee filter. For jelly, clarity is important!

Sterilize the jars and lids (refer to a canning manual). In a stainless-steel pot, stir the lemon juice and sugar into the clear infusion and bring to a full rolling boil that cannot be stirred down. Add the liquid pectin and boil for two more minutes. While boiling, use a handled strainer to skim off foam that rises to the surface, and discard it into a bowl. After the two minutes of boiling, stirring, and skimming, fill and seal the jars, following directions in your canning manual. Let the sealed jars sit undisturbed for six hours to cool, until the lids pop inward (refer to manual).

Well-sealed jars can be stored in a cupboard for up to a year. If the lid of any cooled jar pops both in and out when pressed, either reprocess it in boiling water for ten minutes to attempt a better seal, or store it in the refrigerator and use within three weeks.

Greens, Eggs, and Ham

(4 servings)

1 qt dandelion greens, well washed and tough stems removed
1 ham hock
1 T butter
Salt and pepper to taste

Steep greens in a pot of salted water for about five hours to remove bitterness. Meanwhile, simmer ham shank for about 2 hours; add greens, and cook gently for 45 minutes. Drain; remove ham from bone, and finely chop ham and greens; season with butter, salt, and pepper. Spread over sliced hard-boiled eggs and serve hot.

Dandelion Wine

One of our farmgirl forum members, Michelle Van Dyke, of Rosalia, Washington, sent us two luscious bottles of dandelion and lilac wine this summer, along with this note:

"One of my favorite family stories goes something like this: My mother-in-law sent her husband and children fishing for the day and invited her neighbor over to help bottle up a batch of dandelion wine. Both women are large farmgirls and love to chat. Picture the kitchen—bottles, hoses, and a large crock of wine ready for bottling. When my father-in-law and the kids came home, he looked in the doorway, then tried to keep the kids from seeing what he saw—two women lying on the floor, unable at that point to get up without assistance!"

"My mother-in-law did not give me her secret dandelion wine recipe. The man who gave it to her maybe sixty years ago made her put her hand on the Bible and swear not to give it, so I haven't even asked her beyond that once. I found my recipe online, at Jack Keller's website (winemaking. jackkeller.net/dandelion.asp). He lists over thirty recipes for dandelion wine."

"I ended up using two recipes, then I blended them when it came time to 'age' them. Here are the ingredients (the process is detailed on his website, and does involve learning some wine-making basics, which he also provides). I ended up making the second one when my husband noticed that I didn't put any raisins in. He said his mother always did that. Since the wine was for her, I went picking again."

It gives one a sudden start in going down a barren, stony street, to see upon a narrow strip of grass, just within the iron fence, the radiant dandelion, shining in the grass like a spark dropped from the sun.

– Henry Ward Beecher

Midday Dandelion Wine

(Reprinted with permission)

2   qts dandelion flowers, pulled from open flower clusters
3   lbs granulated sugar
4   navel oranges
1   gal water
Champagne yeast
Yeast nutrient

Dandelion Wine with Raisins

3   qts dandelion flowers, pulled from open flower clusters
1   lb golden raisins
1   gal water
3   lbs granulated sugar
2   lemons
1   navel orange
Champagne yeast
Yeast nutrient

"*Well,* there is time
left—fields everywhere invite
you into them. "
— Mary Oliver

Damsel's Rocket

or Dame's Rocket (*Hesperis matronalis*)

Description

A new plant species has taken up residence on the Palouse, the two-million-acre region where I live. Fittingly called damsel's rocket, this gorgeous "new" breed of flower that comes in luscious hues of purple, lavender, pink, and bright white is shooting up everywhere yonder and yon. She wasn't around when I laid claim to five acres some twenty years ago, and she isn't difficult to tame when need be, so landowners aren't getting out their chemicals. But since she is officially an "invasive" plant and competes for space where native plants might grow, the ecological thing to do when you see her is to invite her into your kitchen. Bordering our fields and ditch banks, she prefers the open and the sunlit, avoiding the shadowy and shady. She stands watch along our back roads, waving as we pass. She'll come into our yards and gardens if we ask her, otherwise she politely declines, leaving a trail of edible tresses wherever she journeys. She's our reminder to be resilient but beautiful, to let our inner wild take root, to gracefully and quietly live in the open.

Chocolate Cream Frosting

Frost your favorite cupcakes with this delicious chocolate frosting, and garnish with fresh damsel's rocket blossoms.

1 1/4 c whipping cream
1/4   c light corn or agave syrup
1/4   c unsalted butter
1   lb semi-sweet or dark chocolate, chopped

Combine cream, syrup and butter in large, heavy saucepan. Whisk over medium heat until mixture begins to simmer. Add chocolate. Reduce heat to low and whisk until frosting is smooth, about 1 minute; transfer to medium-sized bowl. Fill a large bowl with ice. Set bottom of bowl with frosting on top of the ice. Whisk until frosting becomes cool and thickens, about 8 minutes. Place the bowl of frosting on your work surface. Using an electric mixer, beat until color lightens and just until frosting becomes thick enough to hold peaks when beaters are lifted, about 2 minutes (frosting will continue to thicken as it stands). Garnish with flower petals or whole blossoms.

Cattails

Cattails live in a world of their own. In fact, they live where most other plants cannot: in boggy low-lying areas and swamps. Their presence is a sure sign of water. Because every part of the plant can be used for something, they were a staple for Native Americans. The mucilaginous jelly found between its leaves or "swords" in the spring was applied to wounds, the fluff was used for stuffing and warmth, and the dried leaves were woven into baskets and mats.

I have a stand of cattails thirty feet from my door. The part that interests me most is the "asparagus," the tender shoot that forms before the plant flowers. Once peeled, it tastes like a cross between a zucchini and a cucumber—delicious in stir-fry dishes, soups, and salads, or preserved as pickles.

Caution: Young cattails popping up in the spring resemble poisonous plants like the wild iris and daffodil. Since the cattail's cigar-shaped flower clusters are usually evident year-round, look for last year's familiar "brown" cigars within the stand, now whitened and weathered a year later.

Pickled Cattails (one pint jar)

Harvest cattail shoots in early spring when stems are about 10 inches tall. To harvest the shoots, grab the root as low as possible and pull up. Remove the outer leaves and green stem parts, leaving the white heart, which is about 4 inches tall and thinner than your pinkie. Each jar of pickles will contain about two dozen cattail hearts, so harvest accordingly.

2   doz cattail shoots
3/4 c white vinegar
1/4 c lemon juice
1   t salt

Clean cattail shoots and pack into a hot, sterilized jar. Bring remaining ingredients to boil and pour into jar, leaving 1/2-inch headspace. Process for 10 minutes.

WILDERNESS Safety

Whenever you head out into the backcountry, you're taking a risk. From weather to wild animals (and worse yet, weird people), certain dangers are inherent in outdoor travel. But there's no sense in staying inside biting your nails; after all, risk is the very foundation of adventure. The trick is to be prepared for threatening circumstances so that you can relax and enjoy your trip.

One of your most important safety preparations will be writing an itinerary to leave with someone you trust. This is not just a set of willy-nilly destination ideas, it's your lifeline, so plan carefully and stick to it. Be sure to include your route, dates of absence, vehicle description and license plate number, the names of travel companions, and a list of your gear and clothing. If you're late returning from an outing, rescue officials won't know to begin a search unless someone reports you as overdue.

Survival experts recommend every hiker take along three backpacking essentials: a knife, a lighter, and a large, heavy-duty trash bag. The trash bag can serve as a rain jacket or an insulating layer (put it on and stuff it with leaves or grass), or it could also be used as a makeshift water container. Other important items to pack include: water, a detailed map of the area, a compass, some high-energy snacks, rain gear, warm clothes, whistle, mirror, first-aid kit, flashlight, and water treatment pills. A waterproof reflective survival blanket can also come in handy; it's cheap, reusable, and takes up very little space in your pack. A can of bear spray can offer an effective deterrent against both animal and human predators. (Counter Assault Pepper Spray is available online at www.counterassault.com and at REI, www.rei.com.)

You can't depend on your cell phone in the wilderness because coverage can be patchy or nonexistent, but bring it just in case. Moving around or climbing to the top of a peak can increase your chances of finding a signal. A cool feature of cell phones manufactured after 2005 is location identification technology called GPS—Global Positioning System. When you dial 911 from your cell, a public safety answering point can locate where you are within sixty yards! The only caveat is that in order for the GPS service to work, your phone must be within your service area. Contact your service provider for more details before planning your expedition.

GPS and Rescue Devices

If the modern backpacker listened to all the hype about essential gear, they'd essentially have a backpack overflowing with nonessentials. There's a be"wild"ering array of gear to sort through these days, but there is one gadget I probably should have had thirty years ago when I was camping and climbing mountains alone.

A Personal Locator Beacon that sends a signal via satellite in case of an emergency ranks high on my list of necessities, especially if you camp alone. A personalized signal tells rescuers who you are and where you are anywhere on the planet. But it's only to be used in situations of grave danger, when all other means of self-rescue have been exhausted. And don't forget, nothing electronic is a substitute for common sense and wilderness savvy. Gadgets can't think or solve problems, and like anything electronic, they can be subject to failure or coverage can be spotty. And they're spendy—about $400 (www.rei.com).

Weather

Sudden changes in weather can catch you off guard, so it's important to be prepared for all possible weather conditions in your area. Take shelter as soon as you see dark storm clouds gathering, feel the wind pick up, or hear thunder in the distance—but don't stand under a tree. If lightning strikes a tree, electricity will run down the trunk and can ignite a fire. If you're at high elevation, move downslope and head for a building, your car, or even a cave or rock overhang to wait out the storm. Remember that dangerous flash floods can occur in even small ravines and creek beds, so don't huddle up in a drainage area. Stream crossings during high water can also be hazardous, so it's best to stay put until the water drops. If you must cross a waterway, be sure to choose a shallow spot as far from rapids or falls as possible. Use a sturdy stick for stability, and face upstream while crossing.

Hypothermia

Hypothermia (dangerously low body temperature) is the number one killer in the outdoors. It can occur quickly if you're wet and cold, but it can also happen slowly as a result of prolonged exposure to cold, rain, and wind. Early signs are hard to detect, so if you or a companion is at risk, watch for poor judgment, lethargy, shivering, clumsiness. Ward off hypothermia by wearing wool or synthetic layers—NOT cotton, which retains moisture. Don a cap and rain gear before you get drenched. Avoid cold wind exposure, especially when wet (even from sweating).

> " I would feel more optimistic about a bright future for man if he spent less time proving that he can outwit Nature and more time tasting her sweetness and respecting her seniority.
>   – E. B. White "

Strangers

Awareness is the most crucial line of defense when it comes to strangers, and I advise arming yourself with a cell phone or radio and a can of pepper spray. While guns are useful tools of protection, they are too easily used against you if you're not a skilled shooter. For safety, it's always best to hike with a buddy; two people are more intimidating to approach than one, and if one of you is in trouble, the other may be able to get help. If you encounter a stranger who makes you feel uncomfortable for any reason, trust your instincts and move out of the area as quickly as possible. Don't camp near roads; creeps are generally lazy and drive around looking for trouble. And as pleasant as camping near

A Global Positioning System (GPS device) isn't all that necessary, although it could also turn into a life-saving device as long as you know how to use it to navigate your way to safety. About two million GPS units were sold last year in North America, in large part because they became half as expensive and a whole lot easier to use.

My pick just happens to be the least expensive so far. The Lowrance Ifinder Expedition Color costs about $300 (www.thegpsstore.com). It also has a MP3 player that I can't or won't figure out how to use. If you can't leave your music behind, you may as well stay home and watch a nature program on TV. What I do like about this unit is the internal microphone to store messages. For an idea-kind-of-gal like me, I'm rarely without a way to record my next best idea—the one so grand I might forget what it was. If you can't afford a GPS device, I'm here to tell you I survived just fine using good old fashioned topographical maps for many years, although GPS devices might just make them extinct someday.

Now, what about batteries? Battery buying has become about as confusing as the cold cereal aisle in a grocery store … too many choices! I like rechargeable batteries best. I've also learned it's an old wives' tale to store batteries in your refrigerator (it doesn't prolong their life and may actually cause damage), and you mustn't mix regular and rechargeable, or for that matter put new batteries in with old. For a disposable battery that lasts the longest, reach for Energizer Titanium. *Consumer Reports* ranked them No. 1 among alkaline batteries. Top of the line are lithium batteries as opposed to alkaline. They last even longer. For more details, try www.batteryuniversity.com. All depleted batteries should be recycled. To find out how, call 1-877-2-recycle or log on to www.call2recycle.org.

Snake River Canyon, 1978

LOOKING BACK ...

The list of outpost jobs I've held is long, but one of the most remote jobs I ever held wasn't in a designated wilderness area. I had posted a "work wanted" ad on the bulletin board of a small laundromat in the tiny town of Grangeville, Idaho: "Remote job wanted. Will rope/ride/milk your critters, build fence, cook. References."

A 30,000 acre cattle ranch in the Snake River Canyon responded via mail. I accepted and then drove to my new job as a ranch hand in my '53 Ford pickup, traveling three hours on dirt roads that switched back down into the remote Salmon River Gorge, then back up again onto the remote Joseph Plains, and then back down again into the Snake River Canyon just below Hell's Canyon. The saying "steep as a cow's face" took on new meaning. Once winter set in, the only way out was by jet boat along the Snake River, a four-hour trip into Lewiston, Idaho. (I only went out once that year, and along the way, the captain of the boat stopped repeatedly to check his trap lines, tossing in the occasional dead beaver and muskrat.) Our mail and

a rushing stream or breaking waves can be, the sounds of water impair your hearing, so you might not be aware of approaching footsteps. If you're threatened by a stranger, yell at the top of your lungs. There may be someone nearby who can come to your aid, but even if there isn't, the possibility may discourage an attacker. Acting aggressively can also work in your favor. The more troublesome you are (screaming, kicking, punching, biting), the less appealing you are as a target. Even if you avoid confrontation with a stranger, be sure to report any crime, harassment, or suspicious behavior to the local authorities.

Cougars

Cougars are actually very elusive creatures; they'd prefer to avoid contact with people as much as possible. But, because they are a large and potentially dangerous predator, it's best to be on the safe side if you see one. Stop and stay calm. Don't turn your back or run. Instead, face the animal, stand upright, talk calmly, and try to appear larger. (For example, open your jacket and raise your arms.) If you've got small children with you, pick them up so they won't panic or make rapid movements. If the cougar becomes aggressive, respond aggressively toward it. Shout, wave your arms, or throw nearby objects like rocks and sticks. And, in the rare event of a cougar attack, you should fight back, hitting or kicking tender spots like the animal's eyes, nose, ears, or belly.

Bears

Like cougars, bears generally prefer to avoid people, but they are more likely to investigate the smell of anything edible. Bears that have become accustomed to finding human food in camping areas can become aggressive, leading to attacks on humans and/or the bear being killed by wilderness officials, so minimize bear encounters by keeping a clean camp and storing your food properly. All food (including canned and dehydrated); garbage; and scented toiletries like toothpaste, deodorant, sunscreen, and even lip balm should be kept in bear-resistant containers or hung from trees—at least twelve feet high and ten feet away from the nearest tree trunk—twenty-four hours a day. Never store food in your tent or backpack, and avoid cooking or eating in your tent. Wash dirty dishes immediately, and dispose of waste water at least two hundred feet from your campsite. Pack out all uneaten food, food wrappers, and other garbage in bear canisters (see below).

If a bear does venture into your camp, don't give up your food unless there is imminent risk of injury. Instead, bang pots and pans and yell to discourage the animal's curiosity. If the bear is aggressive, by all means leave camp and report the incident to the authorities. Be aware that in some parks, if your food is not properly stored, it may be confiscated and a fine may be issued to protect other visitors, property, and the bears.

Bear canisters are lightweight, cylindrical containers designed specifically to be animal-proof. They are the best way to secure food, garbage, and other scented items from bears and other wildlife—coolers, garbage cans, and other containers are no match for an inquisitive bear. Canisters are available for loan at some park ranger stations (they may request a small donation), and are now required in many backcountry areas, especially along coastlines and at high altitudes where trees are scarce and it's not possible to hang food properly. You can buy your own bear canisters online at Backpackers' Cache (www.backpackerscache.com) and Wild Ideas (www.wild-ideas.net).

In several wilderness camping areas, bear wires for hanging food have been installed between trees. They're usually located in centralized areas for several sites to share. Most wires are equipped with cables for attaching and raising food containers off the ground, but it's a good idea to bring 75 to 100 feet of extra rope just in case.

To use the bear wire system, secure your bear canisters in a bag with a looped handle. Unfasten the clip from a ring at the base of the tree, and lower the wire (like a flagpole) until the upper clip is within reach of your bag handle. Fasten the clip onto food bag handle, then raise food bag by pulling the wire, and refasten the lower clip at the base of the tree.

Snakes

Few hikers fall victim to snake bites, but snakes still seem to strike fear in even the most level-headed people. With a little education and caution, you can reduce the chances of injury to yourself and any snakes you may encounter. Remember, snakes are an integral part of the natural ecosystem, and like most animals they will only attack if threatened or startled. Given the chance, they'd prefer just to slither away. Avoid surprising snakes by watching where you step. While traveling at night, keep a flashlight trained on the trail ahead of you. Don't disturb large stones, logs, or branches unless you have to, and then proceed carefully, as these are places that provide shelter for snakes. If you do see a snake, be calm and

groceries were delivered once a week via that same boat.

The outbuildings (I lived in the bunkhouse) and the main house were like museums, outfitted with everything from hand-crank washing machines to manual drill presses. I felt I had seriously stepped back in time and loved the challenge of living again without electricity, phone, TV, and cars—just cows and fences and wide-open spaces.

The ranch had two functional residences. I started out living "on top" of the plains, but once it started to feel like winter was setting in, we abandoned that compound and headed down into the warmer canyon via a jeep and horseback, where the cows would have winter range. The year I worked there, we ended up leaving "summer camp" later than desired because the ranch boss's wife gave birth two weeks late. That meant we "drove" the cows down into the canyon in a blinding snowstorm. Not only did I learn how to assist in the delivery of calves, I assisted in her delivery along with a midwife who, thankfully, knew more about home deliveries than I did.

When spring came, I decided to leave to spend time with my family in Utah. But I barely made it out because of muddy roads, despite tire chains. I had my treadle sewing machine in the back and new job possibilities on the horizon, but I didn't get far. Right after I arrived back in Grangeville, one of the old-timers who lived way out there was thrown off her horse, busting thirty-two bones. Her husband asked if I'd come back out to "the plains" to pick up where she'd left off and also to help nurse her back to health. He picked me up in town, treadle in tow, and off to the Joseph Plains I went again. It is a place of stunning beauty. My daydreams have it still exactly the way it was, lost in time, but waiting for my return.

Getting "Out There" Together

Getting outside can be easier, and a whole lot more fun, if you're equipped with know-how and a group of gal pals to go with. If you'd like to learn new skills and meet other outdoorsy women, check out three national organizations that have local chapters across the country. Join in, gather up, and go wild!

Women in the Outdoors

An outreach of the National Wild Turkey Federation, Women in the Outdoors has eighteen regional coordinators and a quarterly magazine. At events throughout North America, women receive expert instruction as they try camping, hiking, fishing, kayaking, shooting, boating, and bird watching.
www.womenintheoutdoors.org

Becoming an Outdoors-Woman

Becoming an Outdoors-Woman is an outdoor skills program that offers women from all backgrounds a chance to become more competent, confident, and aware in a supportive, non-competitive environment. More than 20,000 women ages 18 to 80+ attend BOW events every year. Workshops introduce women to hunting and shooting, fishing, and non-harvest sports like canoeing and camping. New "Beyond BOW" events include actual pheasant, turkey, or deer hunts; guided fly fishing; caving excursions; sea kayaking; horse packing trips, and more.
www.uwsp.edu/cnr/bow

Women Outdoors

This national organization offers a wide range of activities for all levels of experience and ambition. Women Outdoors members hone outdoor skills, leadership potential, and environmental awareness alongside other women who share similar interests and goals.
www.women-outdoors.org

back away slowly, keeping an eye open for others that might be nearby. Sudden movements like throwing rocks at a snake will only frighten it and incite aggressive behavior. Just offer enough space for both of you to move on unharmed.

Bite Treatment:

Often, snake bites do not result in venom injection, but if you are bitten by a snake, stay calm. The best treatment option is to lie down and stay still. Remove any jewelry or tight-fitting clothing and allow the bite to bleed freely for 30 seconds. Lightly wrap a bandage above and below the wound to slow down circulation of the poison (if you can't get two fingers under the bandage, it's too tight). If you have access to ice or cold water, make a cold pack and place it on the wound. Immobilize the bitten limb and keep it lower than heart level if possible. Don't drink alcohol or take any medicine, and try to get to a medical facility within three hours. Once there, describe the snake as well as possible. Don't attempt the old "cut and suck" method; it's dangerous and ineffective.

Getting Lost

As is true in most hazardous situations, keeping calm is key if you find yourself lost. Common sense is way more important than physical strength and high-tech equipment. As counterintuitive as it may seem, staying in one place makes you much easier to find. Take measures to keep warm and dry, and create signals visible from the air such as bright clothing in a forest clearing or a flashing mirror. Building a fire is a good way to alert searchers, but use caution when burning in dry timber during hot summer months. If you're aware of a forest burn ban, stick to other signaling techniques. The hard part is waiting anywhere from hours to days for rescuers to find you, but your patience and persistent signaling will pay off.

Wilderness First Aid

Proper preparation for wilderness emergencies is more important than any item you can pack in a first aid kit. The fact is, if you have the requisite gear, knowledge, and training, you probably won't need to use them. It's a great idea to take a first aid and CPR course before your trip to hone your emergency skills. After all, what good is a well-stocked kit if you don't know how to use it? Try to find a wilderness-oriented course if you can. A good place to find information on first aid courses is through your local Red Cross.

The "Leave No Trace" Fire

When you're camping in pristine or easily damaged areas like alpine or tundra, a new-fangled accessory called a fire blanket can help you make a fire without scarring the environment. This heat-treated fiberglass mat is lightweight and flexible so that it's easily packed and carried. All you have to do is cover the blanket with one to two inches of soil, then build your fire. The blanket contains ash and insulates the ground from heat. When you extinguish your fire, you pack out the soil and ashes in the blanket and dispose of them elsewhere.

Getting "Up There" Together

For a top-notch outing with friends, it's good to think lofty thoughts. Renting a Forest Service lookout tower will surely give you that thigh-and-calf burning workout you've been wanting, www.firelookout.org.

Libby Langston never forgot how good it felt when she first visited a lookout tower in 1985, her friend waving from the catwalk of her cozy little summer home on very tall legs. Her love for lookouts compelled her to create a book that would honor these historic structures and raise money for their continued restoration and management.

The *Lookout Cookbook* isn't just a cookbook. Full of stunning historic photos, it tells the stories of women like Mary Byers, who spent nine seasons in the '80s on a lookout in Montana. Mary's "6,000-foot English Muffins" recipe does more than satisfy your taste buds. It fuels the continued preservation of lookouts. Join the Forest Fire Lookout Association (www.firelookout.org), where you can purchase the cookbook and learn how to participate in a restoration project.

Safe Water
IN THE WILD

Finding Water

When you're backpacking miles from the comforts of civilization, you simply can't carry enough water to keep you properly hydrated, much less cook and clean with. A hiker needs to drink at least a gallon per day—more if she's going at a vigorous pace in hot weather—and at eight pounds per gallon, that adds up! If you're packing dehydrated foods, you'll also need water for them as well. The bottom line: water is a precious commodity, and you've got to know how to get it far from home. Fortunately, finding water is possible in virtually any wilderness environment; you just have to know where to look.

By far the best tool for locating water is your topographical (topo) map. Almost any good-sized, year-round water source will be marked on a topo map, so you can pinpoint your water sources before you get out there. But if you stray from your designated path and need to find water, you should still be able to find a place to replenish your supplies.

Start by looking for surface water such as streams, rivers, and lakes. Even when you see no obvious signs of water, there are indicators that can lead you in the right direction.

Watch for:

- **Low-lying areas**, ravines, and valleys into which water naturally drains
- **Rock crevices** where rainwater may collect
- **Muddy or damp ground** (forming a depression in damp soil may allow a bit of water to settle out)
- **Patches of green vegetation** in a dry landscape (they're sourcing nearby water)
- **Animal tracks** (if you find a heavy trail, it probably leads to or from a water source)
- **Birds** such as ducks, geese, herons, egrets, bald eagles, and ospreys, which often stick close to water
- **Insects**, particularly mosquitoes, may indicate a marshy area

Collecting Water

If you can't find surface water, don't let desperation dehydrate you. You can sustain yourself in a wilderness survival situation by collecting water from the atmosphere or from plants.

Rain: Collect rainwater in bottles, cups, pans, or bowls as it flows off the roof of your tent or even tree branches. This method accumulates water faster than simply setting a container out to catch rain as it falls from the sky.

Snow and Ice: Melt them before drinking. Eating snow or sucking on ice saps energy, reduces body temperature, and actually increases dehydration.

Dew: Collect morning dew by setting a cloth in long, wet grass. When the cloth is soaked, wring it out directly into your mouth or a container.

Condensation: Tie a plastic bag over a green tree or shrub branch with exposure to the sun (take care not to puncture the bag). Close the bag tightly, leaving a small opening at the bottom above the mouth of an open container. Evaporation from the leaves or needles will produce condensation in the bag that will drip into the container.

OUTSPOKEN...

Jean Motzer, age sixty-seven, is a born-and-bred mountain woman. She grew up in Leadville, Colorado, the highest incorporated town in the United States, and now lives in Denver, barely an hour from the high country where she continues to hike, climb, and snowshoe.

"I love all the civilized 'goodies' my city offers, but I know that my spirit withers if all I have are bricks and blacktop, manicured lawns, and stores full of things to buy. I must get to where my primary consciousness is the sun (sometimes rain or snow!) on my face, the wind in the trees, the rocky trail underfoot, the scent of moist trees, the occasional meeting with a deer, the gamble that I will summit and get back down into the trees without being struck by lightning! Without fail, for years and years, when I go to the altitude where the trees cannot grow and the tiny amazing flowers hug the hostile soil, literally for dear life, I hear a voice within saying, 'You're home, Jean. This is where you belong.'"

Jean has climbed thirty of Colorado's "14ers" (14,000-foot peaks), and she aspires to summit all fifty-four. "I'm not sure my knees and reflexes are up to the challenge," she says. "But one day, one peak at a time—right?"

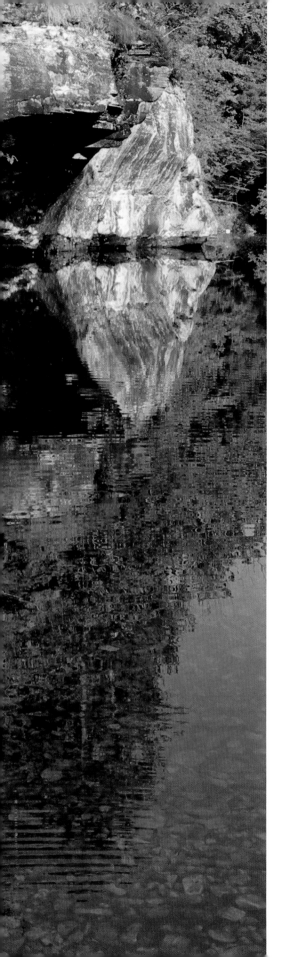

Purification

Dipping your hands into a cool, crisp stream and drinking what nature has to offer seems like an idyllic means of communing with the outdoors, but when it comes to water, practicality and backcountry know-how are essential. Wild water sources (lakes, rivers, and even springs and glacial runoff) can be contaminated with bacteria, parasites, and other microscopic creepy-crawlies that have the potential to cause severe gastrointestinal troubles and disease. So, how can you have your wilderness water and drink it too?

Purifying water is the solution. There are three methods of purification that make water safe to drink: boiling, iodination, and filtration. Each has pros and cons, depending on your situation.

• Boiling is great because it's simple, low-tech, and it destroys all disease-causing microbes. Simply bring a pot of water to a rolling boil for three minutes, and it's safe to drink. But, boiling does require a good bit of fuel, effort, and time (waiting for water to boil, then waiting for it to cool). The other issue with boiling is it doesn't filter out silt, leaves, and the like. An unbleached coffee filter works well for "clearing up" water before boiling.

• Iodination requires iodine crystals or tablets, which are lightweight and effective against most microbes except Crypto-sporidium bacteria, which wreaks havoc on the gastrointestinal system and has no cure (it'll run its course in seven to ten miserable days). Also, iodine tablets make your water taste pretty bad, and the process can be time-consuming. For example, purification takes at least ten minutes if the water is warm, and it can take up to eight hours if the water is cold or murky. Adding Vitamin C to the water will "drop" some of the iodine out of the solution, making the taste much more acceptable, but be sure you've allowed time for purification to occur so that the Vitamin C doesn't interfere with the effect of the iodine. And again, even though iodine kills anything dangerous, it doesn't filter out floating bits of stuff, so keep those coffee filters handy. Potable Aqua brand iodine tablets are available at REI (www.rei.com). Note: Pregnant women and people with thyroid conditions should not use iodine to purify water.

• Filtration works by moving water through a special filter that removes dangerous organisms such as bacteria and the cysts of parasites. Filtration also improves taste by removing any organic material that might be floating around, and an activated charcoal

element within the filter will neutralize tastes and odors. Because no filter has pores small enough to trap viruses, many filters also incorporate iodine within the filter as an added purifier. The trouble with any filter is that it eventually clogs up. The dirtier the water, the quicker it clogs. Some filters have prefilters designed to catch sediment before it reaches the microfilter. Either way, you'll end up cleaning or replacing the filter element (bring replacements in case you get clogged in the field). Filters are also slow to use and cost more than the other purification options.

When choosing a filter, consider:
• the"absolute" pore size, which should be one micron or less to catch bacteria, protozoa, and cysts (you may need a small pore size in virus-prone places)
• iodine purifying element
• ease of cleaning in the field
• weight
• cost
• pumping speed

There are about thirteen models available at REI, ranging from the basic Katadyn Micro Filter Water Bottle for $34.95 to the deluxe Katadyn Pocket Filter with Output Hose for $220. A great feature on the REI website is that you can select different models to compare features and performance. Note: Make sure to take your filter's directions into the field with you!

Bottles and Canteens

In times past, the Chumash Indians of California used tightly woven baskets as water vessels. They could even boil water in these baskets by adding heated rocks! Twined basket "bottles" were used as canteens. Less tightly woven, these were coated with asphaltum, or pine pitch, to make them watertight. Other tribes throughout North America used clay, birch bark, and animal skin vessels for transporting water.

These days, most water bottles are made of plastic. Sure, plastic is convenient, but it's a non-renewable resource, it's not biodegradable, and it has toxic ramifications. Plastics used in many water containers leach dangerous chemicals into their contents that have been linked to a host of health hazards like cancer, chromosomal disruption, miscarriages, liver and kidney damage, and birth defects. Check the bottom of your bottles for a symbol that shows a number inside a triad of arrows. Plastics numbered 2, 4, and 5 are considered safe so far, but given all of

Make Your Own Water Filter

This last-ditch plan doesn't guarantee bacteria-free water, but it's better than no filter at all. Stick to clear, cold, flowing water if possible.

Materials:
• an empty container for the filter (plastic bottles are perfect)
• knife
• grass, sand, and small rocks
• a second container to catch your filtered water

Instructions:
1. Cut off the bottom of the filter container.
2. Holding the container upside down, loosely plug the smaller opening at the bottom with grass or other plant material (this will help keep sand from washing through into your drinking water).
3. Add layers of rocks and sand, alternating coarse and fine layers. Don't worry if the sand spills down and hides the gravel layers (as shown in photo).
4. Collect some water in your hands (or a third container), and pour it slowly through the cut-off end of your filter. Catch the water from below in your second container. The water should drip from the filter slowly, and it should be clear. If not, you may need to pour the water through the filter again.

MaryJane, wilderness ranger, Uintas, 1974

Red Castle, Uintas

When I worked as a Wilderness Ranger in the Uintas, I lived in the shadow of this mountain, called Red Castle, and *yep!* I did climb to the top of it once. At its base was a three-hundred-acre teal-blue lake that provided me with all the fish I could eat.

the negatives associated with plastics, I'd like to give you a couple of other options to consider. (If the number is anything other than 2, 4, or 5, I recommend recycling it.)

Glass is a great choice when portability isn't an issue—it's natural, biodegradable, and inert. If you're picnicking or car camping, you can bring gallon glass bottles along with just a bit of extra care when packing. Old glass juice jugs are heavy-duty and have screw-on tops, so they travel really well. Canning jars can double as eco-friendly camp cups to be washed and reused.

If you're hiking, climbing, or cycling, though, you're in the market for an unbreakable vessel. Klean Kanteen (www.kleankanteen.com) offers a line of reusable, lightweight bottles made from #304 stainless steel, the material of choice in the food processing, dairy, and brewery industries. According to Klean Kanteen, their stainless steel bottles are easy to clean, durable, inert, sanitary, toxin-free, and non-leaching. Klean Kanteens are available in 12, 18, 27, and 40-ounce sizes, equipped with your choice of a stainless steel flat cap, loop cap, or a sport drinking cap made of polypropylene plastic (#5).

Dehydration

Dehydration occurs when your body loses water faster than you can replace it, and it can happen in any climate. You lose up to one gallon of water each day through normal sweating and urination, more if you are hot or exercising strenuously. If you don't replenish this water, you can become dangerously dehydrated.

We tend to assume that thirst will alert us to dehydration, but this isn't always the case. It's possible to lose fluid so quickly that our thirst mechanism is overwhelmed or overridden. If you're running low on water, it's critical to watch for other symptoms of dehydration, including decreased coordination, cramping, fatigue, irritability, anxiety, lightheadedness, and impairment of judgment. Also, check your urine whenever you make a pit stop. A healthy person getting adequate fluids will produce about four cups of urine every twenty-four hours, so if you're under that amount and your pee is dark yellow, you are definitely dehydrated. At this point, you've got to take steps to stop losing water and rehydrate, because severe dehydration can result in shock or loss of consciousness, requiring immediate medical attention.

Slow down sweating by removing clothing, finding shade, or dipping into a creek. Avoid heavy foods and alcohol, which use up fluids. Rehydrate gradually by drinking water. It's not necessary to chug a bunch of sports drinks touting "electrolyte replenishment." Electrolytes are natural chemicals in our body fluids that supply electrical energy necessary for nerve and muscle functions; they are depleted along with water when we perspire, and there's no way to regain them instantaneously. If you try to replace lost fluids all at once, you can end up with water intoxication, officially called dilutional hyponatremia, which amounts to dangerously diluted blood sodium levels. If you try to replace, in equal amounts, all the electrolytes you've lost, hormonal triggers can cause gastric distress, swelling, muscle spasms, and cramping. In short, it's a lot easier—and better for your health—to stay hydrated than to try to recalibrate after pushing beyond your limits.

MaryJane, wilderness ranger, Uintas, 1974

How to Stay Hydrated:

- **Drink water** and snack often throughout the day to keep hydrated and maintain optimum electrolyte levels.
- **Rest often**, preferably in the shade.
- **Wear clothing** that allows air flow to your skin and a brimmed hat.
- **Keep your mouth closed** to retain moisture.
- **Suck on a hard candy** or even a pebble to keep your mouth moist.
- **Don't wait** until you run out of water to look for more!

"A sure way to avoid housework ... live outdoors!"

– Eren
MaryJanesFarm Farmgirl Connection
www.maryjanesfarm.org

bugOFF!

One of the most effective repellents for biting bugs is plain old sulfur. It works better than most commercial products and doesn't contain harsh artificial chemicals. Powdered sulfur, called sublimed sulfur or flowers of sulfur, is available from most pharmacies (though you might have to special order it). Put the powder in a salt shaker or an old sock and dust it around on your pants, socks and boots. The yellow-colored powder has a slight stinky smell, but it won't stain your clothing and washes out easily. Sulfur may irritate the skin, so try it on a small area of your skin first, and try to keep it on the outside of your clothes. One bottle costs about $12 and can last a family of four for a year.

Three commercially-made products that have great reputations for safety and effectiveness are:

• **Quantum Buzz Away Extreme:** Spray bottle or towelette wipes combine essential plant oils with soy bean and geranium oil for lasting natural protection. www.quantumhealth.com

• **Crocodile! Herbal Insect Repellent:** Made from organically grown rosemary, peppermint, and thyme, it can be used on pets too. www.mosquitosolutions.com/crocodile

• **Repel Lemon Eucalyptus:** Oil of lemon eucalyptus has been recommended by the Centers for Disease Control and Prevention for effective protection against mosquitoes that may carry West Nile virus. www.repel.com

Some people swear by simple home remedies such as pure vanilla bean extract, garlic, lemon juice, or sulfur powder. Everyone's body chemistry is different, so a bit of trial and error will confirm what works best for you. Note: Don't use concentrated essential oils while pregnant / nursing or on children under three years of age.

NATURE'S NASTIES

Not even the most devout outdoorswoman can deny that nature has a nasty side, fraught with itches and ouches galore. There are actually places in America where a vista of gorgeous wilderness can look more like a nightmare through a midsummer haze of mosquitoes. Worse yet, as you're swatting the mosquitoes, you're also trying to scratch chigger-ridden ankles, which might just send you tumbling headlong into a patch of poison ivy. Yikes! It's a scary prospect, but don't let the heebie-jeebies keep you locked up indoors till the deep freeze of winter. If you know what to look out for and how to steer clear of nature's nasties, you can enjoy the open air safely and comfortably all year long.

CHIGGERS

Also known as harvest mites, chiggers are tiny soft-bodied insects that live in grassy, brushy, or wooded areas in temperate, humid climates. The irritating larval mites creep around close to the ground until a warm body wanders through the weeds. Contrary to popular belief, chiggers do not burrow into the skin. They pierce the skin and inject enzymes that digest skin cells for consumption, causing severe itching and swelling. Chiggers generally target body parts where the skin is thin and moist: ankles, thighs, groin, waistline, or wrists. They stay in one spot up to four days, feeding until they're full and then dropping off to complete their life cycle.

ticks

Ticks are small arachnids that feed exclusively on blood from other animals. They are found in grass, weeds, and brush, ready and waiting to crawl onto a host. They attach themselves to exposed skin with a barbed structure in their mouth area called a hypostome, which is why they're so difficult to remove. Because ticks transmit serious diseases such as Lyme disease, tularemia, and Rocky Mountain spotted fever, it is important to remove them promptly. The longer an infectious tick feeds, the greater the chance of disease transmission. Carry white masking tape or a pet hair roller to "blot" ticks from your clothes and skin while in the field, and then check your entire body for ticks immediately after leaving the woods. Remove embedded ticks by grasping them with tweezers as close to your skin as possible. Pull slowly and steadily. Crushing or irritating the tick (with heat or chemicals) can cause it to regurgitate its stomach contents into the skin, increasing the possibility of infection.

MOSQUITOES

It's the females of the species that have a taste for blood. Both male and female mosquitoes feed on nectar, but the female will also drink blood to supplement her protein needs during the development and laying of her eggs. When she lands on a host, she injects a mild anesthetic agent which masks the pain of the "bite." Then, she pokes her needle-like mouthparts into the skin and drinks her fill. Her saliva is teeming with digestive enzymes and anticoagulants that cause an itchy reaction.

In many cases, the more a person gets bitten, the worse the swelling and itching. But some lucky people actually become insensitive and show no reaction at all! Other people become increasingly allergic with repeated stings. Watch out for mosquitoes at dawn, dusk, and throughout the night when mosquitoes are most active. Also, mosquitoes congregate around slow and stagnant water, so avoid lingering in marshy areas.

PESKY PLANTS

Poison ivy, oak, and sumac are three of nature's nastiest plants. Poison ivy is the biggest troublemaker because the entire plant, minus the pollen, is toxic year-round—yep, even the stems can get you in the winter after the leaves drop. The severity of the rash you get from any of these plants depends on your sensitivity to their oily resin. It dries quickly on anything it touches and can spread to skin from clothing, shoes, pet fur, and more.

Worse than touching a poisonous plant, though, is breathing the resin in campfire smoke. Inhaling the smoke can cause life-threatening lung inflammation, so don't pitch these plants into the fire.

The best thing you can do if you come in contact with poison ivy, oak, or sumac along the trail is to wash your skin immediately with rubbing alcohol, which you can pack in the form of lightweight swabs. Soap works, too, but not as well. Be sure to rinse well with cold water; hot water can open your pores to the oil and worsen the reaction.

There are all sorts of topical treatment options, from cider vinegar to aloe to tea tree oil, but a cool compress is as soothing a solution as you're likely to find—just don't scratch!

> **If you think** you are too small to be effective, you have never been in bed with a mosquito.
>
> – Betty Reese

OUTSPOKEN...

Tia Forrest, mother of five and grandmother of three, has always loved working in the outdoors. "I have been a firefighter, dispatcher, landscaper, and for the last five years, a roofer—and I love it!" She says it is her love of the outdoors and all its wonders that inspired her to create a line of herbal salves called "The Healing Forrest."

"My mother, and her mother as well, preferred remedies they had control over, so it was natural for me to know these firsthand. My interest in plants started in high school botany class, but really blossomed when I started having children," Tia says. "Reading the labels of baby creams, I found I couldn't pronounce the ingredients, and when I asked my doctor and he couldn't either, I decided to fall back on my own family's traditions." The Healing Forrest (www.thehealingforrest.com) sprouted, and twenty years later, it's still growing strong.

Tia offers Honey Salve and Honey Putty for burns and skin healing, Comfrey Salve for deep tissue healing, and Cayenne Salve for bleeding and pain relief. She has even developed the "Bug Stick" for soothing insect stings and bites (www.thehealingforrest.com).

"I have always believed that Mother Nature provides everything we need to relieve the bumps and bruises of life; it is a matter of learning to use it."

225

Working IN THE WILD

I've heard it takes a rare breed of woman to work in the wilderness, but I'm not so sure that's true. I believe that any woman who hears the whisper of wild places, who feels that gut-level urge to blaze a trail, has what it takes to work outdoors. And, based on my own experiences, I can tell you there are few jobs as fulfilling. Whether you're inclined to track grizzlies in Yellowstone or pitch in at an out-of-the-way organic farm, the satisfaction is the same. You spend your days challenging your muscles as much as your mind, footloose and free of stuffy office walls. There is a fantastic spiritual awakening that can happen when you earn your living away from society and all its material baggage. It's an exercise in survival, pure and simple.

Some people work in the wild full time, year round; others do it seasonally. The tricky part is actually landing your dream job because outdoor positions are in relatively short supply, and droves of people want them. Keep your eyes open for people who are doing things that you'd like to do: camp counselors, wildlife researchers, rafting guides, whatever, and then start making connections. Introduce yourself, ask questions. What sort of education and training do you need? Are apprenticeships available? Can you volunteer? Volunteering is a great way to figure out if a particular position is right for you, and you will also have a leg up if employment opportunities arise.

When I started working for the Forest Service in the 1970s, the agency was still pretty much an old boys' club. I was among the first small group of female wilderness rangers. Naturally, I was

MaryJane, Wilderness Ranger Uintas, 1974

WWOOFing

Ever have an urge to travel the country—or the world—on a shoestring budget? If your idea of adventure includes working hard and getting dirty, WWOOFing might just be your ticket.

Worldwide Opportunities on Organic Farms (www.wwoof.org) is a non-profit network linking volunteer workers with organic farmers. As a WWOOF volunteer, you get to travel dirt-cheap to an organic farm where you work for room and board. Duties and schedules vary, but you will typically put in six-hour days with at least one day off per week. Whether you're milking goats, weeding gardens, creating an alternative energy system, or building a barn, you're guaranteed diverse hands-on learning opportunities. Most hosts are simple self-sustaining family farms, so accommodations tend to be rustic, meals are fresh-off-the-farm, and the atmosphere is all about homegrown hospitality.

Aw, shucks!

August 13, 2007

Dear MaryJane,
I found your mailing address on your amazing website. It validated what I always knew since I first met you: You are an "amazing woman"! Remember that "amazing mile-long buck-and-pole fence" you and your partner built for me at Goosewing Guard Station (was it 1975)? I was up there a few weeks back, and it brought back some good memories in some good country with some good friends. Goosewing hasn't changed much other than Roanie, the packhorse, and Mort, the mule, weren't in the corral. Matter of fact, no use had been made of the cabins this summer. Happy farming!

Al Becker

227

OUTSPOKEN...

When summertime rolls around, **Betsy Kepes** and her family shed the trappings of civilized life in upstate New York and migrate to the Idaho wilderness where they live out of backpacks, working as a seasonal trail maintenance and fire lookout crew.

"We love the combination of outdoor paid work and wilderness exploration," Betsy explains.

She and her husband Tom worked trails during college and were determined to keep it up with their two boys, Lee and Jay, in tow. Lee actually celebrated his first birthday at a remote fire lookout tower in the Selway-Bitterroot Wilderness, and they've been at it ever since. Lee is now twenty, and Jay is twelve.

What's the biggest reward of being an outbound family? "Being together for weeks at a time without normal everyday distractions. Even with the stress of working hard, we feel comfortable and at home in the woods. What can be better than ending a day's work at a high alpine lake, dropping our packs, stripping down, and jumping in for a swim?"

Of course, Betsy admits there can be challenges too. "Jay was seven the first time I put a pack on him, and he was like a horse who had never worn a saddle. He lasted about a mile, and then I carried his pack on top of mine for the rest of the week."

Even though it can occasionally be tough to keep up morale, especially when it's hot, buggy, or pouring down rain, the Kepes family wouldn't have it any other way. "Lying in the tent at night, surrounded by tired, smelly bodies, all of us reading by the light of our headlamps—nothing could be finer."

proud to be paving the way for other outbound gals to follow, but it was also a hefty responsibility—I wanted to live up to the legacy of the few tough women who had come before me. Women like Hallie Daggett.

Eight years after the U.S. Forest Service was established in 1905, 35-year-old Hallie Morse Daggett was hired as the first female forest fire lookout, stationed at the Eddy's Gulch Lookout Station in the Siskiyou Mountains of northern California. For fourteen years, she spent her summers in a little cabin at the top of 6,444-foot Klamath Peak, receiving a whopping salary of $840 per year. Hallie admitted that she'd always dreamed of living in a log cabin, and her lookout suited her perfectly. "Indoors as cozy as could be wished, while outdoors was a grander dooryard than any estate in the land could boast ... What a prospect of glorious freedom from four walls and a time-clock."

According to the agency journal *American Forestry* in 1914, "Some of the Service men predicted that after a few days of life on the peak she would telephone that she was frightened by the loneliness and the danger, but she was full of pluck and high spirit ... she grew more and more in love with the work. Even when the telephone wires were broken and when for a long time she was cut off from communication with the world below she did not lose heart. She not only filled the place with all the skill which a trained man could have shown, but she desires to be reappointed when the fire season opens this year."

Hallie worked at Eddy's Gulch for 14 years, leaving a lasting impression with her dauntless enthusiasm, skill, and steadfast work ethic.

Today, women account for close to 40 percent of Forest Service employees, and they're involved in every aspect of national forest management. In fact, in January of 2007, Montana forester Gail Kimbell became the first woman to head the agency, overseeing 155 national forests, 30,000 employees, and a nearly $5 billion budget. Patricia Riexinger, the first woman to preside over the traditionally male domain of New York's Department of Environmental Conservation, said she "wants to restore a sense of wonder to a public that is out of touch with nature."

It may have taken almost a century, but women have found firm footing in the wild workforce, and we're here to stay.

So, climb the corporate ladder in a natural resource agency or sign up for a summer on an Alaskan fishing boat. The choice is yours. All you have to do is dig in your heels and get to work. If you're not sure where to start, check out the list of job resources on my website, www.maryjanesoutpost.org.

Go, girl—the wild world awaits you.

Helen Dowe climbs the ladder to her lookout tower (above), Devil's Head Lookout, Pike National Forest, Colorado, 1919. Below, Helen readies her horse for her trip to the tower; and upper right, she's on the job scanning for fires.

> " What a prospect of glorious *freedom* from four walls and a time-clock. "

Women and Lookouts

Maybe it's the urge to nest. Possibly it's a bad case of cabin fever (romantic notions about living in a cabin). Perhaps it's the need for a five-star view. Castles in the air. Whatever it is, women have been drawn to the job of lookout towering ever since permanent lookout towers were first built in 1910. By the time I was born, in 1953, there were more than five thousand lookout towers in use; today, there are roughly three hundred. When I landed my dream job on a lookout in 1972, men were still running the agencies that managed them, but they specifically sought women for the job of "overseeing" their entire domain. "Men get antsy and more lonely," I was told by the man who hired me to "man" his tower.

That said, I climbed my hundred-foot tower knowing exactly what it was they really wanted. They wanted someone to "woman" their tower. In the cabin at its base, I cleaned, sewed, baked—I stayed busy. I created routine, standard medicine for keeping the blues at bay.

Ironically, as the Forest Service shuts down many of its lookouts (fire-spotting accomplished now with airplanes), more Americans are able to enjoy them. To find out how you can "be above it all," go to www.firelookout.org.

66 If the sight of the blue skies fills you with joy,

If a blade of grass springing up in the fields
has power to move you,

If the simple things of nature have a message
that you understand,

Rejoice, for your soul is alive. 99

– Eleonora Duse

LOOKING BACK ...

I didn't fully appreciate what happened to me that day long ago when I was a young woman in my twenties. For a long time afterwards, when I tried to wrap some logic around it, I kept shaking my head in disbelief. I think now, some thirty years later, one must allow for magic. Magic happens—no explanation needed.

I'd been walking for two days along the Selway River trail in the Bitterroot Wilderness. Hiking alone, I was in that dreamy state that only walking alone will summon. It was hot, about ninety degrees, but I was drinking plenty of water. (So no, I didn't hallucinate from dehydration.)

It's an amusing image to me today, but I was hiking in a one-piece bathing suit carrying a full backpack, a ten-day trip ahead of me, walled in by a river and solid pine trees. My "outfit" included a fabric kerchief on my head. I'd take off my boots and backpack, then walk into the river frequently to cool off, making sure I drenched my "hat" for refrigeration the next few miles.

Everything in my life felt perfectly right that day. In fact, my brain was almost empty and free of chatter. That's the beauty of hiking alone. Empty. Quiet. Open to magic.

I'd been eating my usual dried fare, crackers, cheese, freeze-dried cottage cheese, pineapple. Coffee. "Wouldn't something fresh taste good right now?" I came around a corner in the trail near Maiden Creek and there stood an apple tree, with a single apple on it. I picked it and bit in. At home, with more apples and more distractions, I might have eaten the apple with my mind on other things. But here, I thought about every bite. I tasted and savored every juicy mouthful. I took my time before every swallow. I ate all of it, even the core, but spit the seeds out, thinking, "This is how this tree got here in the first place."

A month later, I walked that same trail expecting to say hello to that lone apple tree. As I rounded that familiar corner in the trail, I looked for my tree. It wasn't there. It couldn't have been cut down, and a flash flood couldn't have taken it. The only explanation was magic. Hard to swallow, I know, but now I have the magic of it to savor forever.

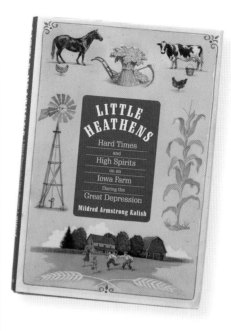

Little Heathens: Hard Times and High Spirits on an Iowa Farm During the Great Depression
by Mildred Armstrong Kalish
Bantam, 2007

Last year, I was honored to be asked to write a back-cover endorsement for *Little Heathens: Hard Times and High Spirits on an Iowa Farm During the Great Depression*. I was entranced by my advance copy and was more than glad to sing its praises:

"Now that cell phones are a way of life, you won't find a better way to participate in the Good Old Days. Whether you are of farm origins or not, Little Heathens *is a bit of history begging to be borrowed. Like a neighborly cup of sugar, it will sweeten your modern-day life."*

Imagine my surprise when I received a copy and found my praises were among the likes of Ted Kooser, U.S. Poet Laureate, 2004–2006; Jim Harrison, author of *Legends of the Fall*; and Joan Silber, author of *Ideas of Heaven: A Ring of Stories*. Turns out we weren't just whistlin' Dixie; in December 2007, the *New York Times Book Review* proclaimed *Little Heathens* to be one of "The 10 Best Books of 2007"!

Books by and for Adventurous Women

Here's a list of inspirational books that will keep your enthusiasm for getting "out there" on track.

A Keeper of Bees: Notes on Hive and Home

by Allison Wallace
Random House, 2006
Somewhere between natural history and memoir, Wallace shares her story of moving to the Arkansas backwoods and building a simple life in the complex company of bees.

A Mile in Her Boots: Women Who Work in the Wild

by Jennifer Bové
Travelers' Tales/Solas House, 2006
Tighten up your bootlaces and head into the backcountry with a diverse and intriguing group of women whose stories run the gamut of on-the-job adventures. Smoke jumping, river running, bear tracking, and cloud collecting are just a few of the occupations detailed in these compelling tales by women on the front lines of wilderness work.

LOOKING BACK ...

In the '70s, when I was working for the Forest Service, I was catching and eating fish every day. I was alone all summer and had some time on my hands. With my bare hands, I decided to challenge my fishing instincts and lay down my pole. I knew of a cold stream above timberline just below a 300-acre cobalt blue lake where some pretty big trout hung out. I discovered that I could nestle among the boulders, hiding my shadow, and hold one of my hands in the creek waiting for a fish to swim by. Quickly, my hand would turn numb from the cold water. Patiently, I would "tickle the tummy" of a fish, grab it, and harvest dinner and breakfast.

One day, I remember watching for hours as a man on horseback slowly worked his way from the top of a mountain down the rocky trail to where I was. When he finally pulled up next to me, I held up my line of fish and proclaimed with pride, "I caught them all with my bare hands!"

Well, as it turns out, he was a Fish and Game officer, and it's illegal to catch a trout with your hands. According to the law, a trout has to willingly bite a hook. Pleading "ignorance of the law" didn't fly either. He confiscated my fish, set up his camp for the night, and ate them all himself. I never heard anything more, so I decided he must have taken heart and dropped the matter.

A year or so later, a Fish and Game officer was featured in a local newspaper. The story was something like, "A Day in the Life of a Fish and Game Officer." Among his duties, he told the reporter, he was trying to find a young woman who once worked for the Forest Service and "serve a warrant for her arrest for a Fish and Game violation." I figured it was me. I turned myself in and was driven several hours to a small Wyoming town where the local judge held court in a laundromat on Main Street. I was fined thirty-five dollars. "Fishy" somehow. "Caught" for sure.

" I caught
them
with my
bare hands! "

Arctic Dance:
The Mardy Murie Story

by Charles Craighead
Graphic Arts Center Publishing
Company, 2002
Full of intimate stories, letters, and photographs, this book invites you on a journey through the adventurous life of conservationist Mardy Murie, whose commitment to saving wild places led to the creation of The Wilderness Society and the Arctic National Wildlife Refuge.

Bold Spirit: Helga Estby's Forgotten Walk Across Victorian America

by Linda Lawrence Hunt
Anchor, 2005
In 1896, Norwegian immigrant and mother of eight Helga Estby was in dire financial straits when a mysterious sponsor offered her $10,000 to walk across America. Armed with ten dollars and a revolver, Helga and her teenage daughter Clara set out on a treacherous and inspirational adventure east from Washington to New York.

Crazy Woman Creek: Women Rewrite the American West

by Linda M. Hasselstrom
Mariner Books, 2004
In this collection of stories and poetry, real western women celebrate the power and promise of gathering together, whether it's at a drugstore, a powwow, or a sewing circle.

Land Circle

by Linda Hasselstrom
Fulcrum Publishing Inc., 2006
The author, a true-grit rancher who embraces the environmental ethic, explores her visceral connection with the land in this collection of her own eloquent essays and poems.

I N D E X

I N D E X

Leaning Into the Wind: Women Write from the Heart of the West

by Nancy Curtis
Mariner Books, 1998
Spanning the high plains, this anthology proves that hardworking women with heart are alive and well. Whether detailing the rigors of ranching or the sentiments of rural family life, each author opens the passenger door of her pickup truck and invites us along for the ride.

Nothing to Do but Stay

by Carrie Young
University of Iowa Press, 2000
In eight spirited essays, Young describes her life as a north plains pioneer daughter in the early 1900s. She relates her mother's bold journey from Minnesota to stake her own land claim before marrying and gives us a unique perspective on growing up in a Norwegian immigrant frontier family.

Peace at Heart: An Oregon Country Life

by Barbara Drake
Oregon State University Press, 1998
In this charming essay collection, Drake shares the tender intimacy she feels for her Oregon farm. She weaves stories and practical farm sense in such engaging prose that, by the end, you feel as if you've visited the idyllic country home of a good friend.

Still Life with Chickens: Starting Over in a House by the Sea

by Catherine Goldhammer
Hudson Street Press, 2006
In a year of profound transition, Goldhammer gets a divorce, forfeits a comfortable paycheck, and relocates to a ramshackle New England cottage to raise her daughter and a half dozen chicks. Suffering the challenges and celebrating the joys, Goldhammer reconstructs her life through hard work and pure love.

Sylvia's Farm: The Journal of an Improbable Shepherd
by Sylvia Jorrin
Bloomsbury USA, 2005
This series of vignettes spans the evolution of an unwitting shepherd who weathers the hardships and embraces the joys of farming to become a well-seasoned herdswoman.

Tough Times, Strong Women: Hundreds of Personal Memories and Photographs Honoring Some of the Common Yet Remarkable Women of the 20th Century
by Mike Beno
Reiman Publications, L.P., 1997
Full of grit and unsung glory, these stories pay heartfelt tribute to the women who held our families and country together during the past century.

Trafficking in Sheep: A Memoir: From Off-Broadway, New York, to Blue Island, Nova Scotia
by Anne Barclay Priest
Countryman, 2006
In this heartwarming memoir, Priest shares how she dared to leave her life as a big city actress to become a simple shepherd in Nova Scotia.

We're in the Mountains, Not Over the Hill: Tales and Tips from Seasoned Women Backpackers
by Susan Alcorn
Shepherd Canyon Books, 2003
Humorous and genuine, this book offers insight into every possible aspect of backpacking for those women who dream of doing it but fear it's too late to start. Anecdotes, insights, and buoyant enthusiasm complement a wealth of practical information.

I N D E X

I N D E X

Wilderness A to Z: An Essential Guide to the Great Outdoors
by Rachel Carley
Fireside, 2001
It's all here: wilderness how-to and where-to, natural history, wild wonders, and the naturalists who have worked to preserve our wild places. Everything you've ever wanted to know but might not have even thought to ask.

Women & Thru-Hiking on the Appalachian Trail
by Beverly "Maine Rose" Hugo
Insight Publishing Company, 2000
In 1995, a determined forty-eight-year-old single mother of two hiked the Appalachian Trail from Georgia to Maine and then set out to share her newfound sense of wisdom with others.

Women of the Harvest: Inspiring Stories of Contemporary Farmers
by Holly Bollinger
Voyageur Press, 2007
Women farmers from around the country share their diverse experiences as farmers, family providers, and everyday heroes whose work is never done. Gorgeous color photographs capture the essence of these hearty women who hold tight to the land even as so many others are leaving.

Woodswoman
by Anne LaBastille
Penguin, 1991
In the 1970s, ecologist Anne LaBastille built herself a log cabin on twenty acres in the Adirondack Mountains, miles from the nearest town. In this book, which is the first in a four-part series, she chronicles her adventures and observations living in the wilderness that would become her lifelong home.

Alone, I am only one drop of water, *together* we are blessed rain.

MaryJane, 1958

Carol, 1960

" *If you carry* your childhood with you, you never become older. **"**
– Tom Stoppard

As I wrote this book, my third so far, I found it difficult to stay put and "git 'er done." The wild ways of my past tugged hard, real hard. It was all I could do to cross the finish line. The Tetons called, Hell's Canyon begged, the Selway River pleaded, "Come and be alone with us again." Every creek I'd ever fished, mountain I'd climbed, or lake I'd bathed in said, "Come back."

A book is an undertaking that only another author can completely comprehend—a single recipe that takes a week before you finally nail it, a photograph that takes a month before you get the lighting just so, a sentence late at night that just won't come.

When it's all said and done and a year's worth of work and loose ends are condensed into a mere 240 pages, you get to sit back and write the finale, the THANK YOU!

For editing, I'd like to thank Carol Hill, my daughter Megan Rae (I trust her instincts on writing more than anyone's), Jennifer Bové, and Pam Krauss. I am especially grateful to Will Pitkin, a retired English professor, one of my shareholders, and also a dear friend. Thank you for helping me navigate the world of words in a playful way. For the book's design, I'd like to thank Carol Hill. Her attention to detail, her creativity, her stick-to-it-iveness is nothing short of genius. And somehow, she always finds something positive to say—her infectious laugh and mirthful spirit have been a lifeline to me more than once. For illustrations, I want to thank Gabe Gibler and Anastasia Kovgan, Tom Bowman, and sisters Rita and Sophie Bové. Someday I'd like to put away my camera and create a book that is illustrated with drawings rather than photographs. I love supporting their work! For help with photographs, I thank Jennifer Bové; Erik Jacobson; my son-in-law, Lucas Rae; my daughter, Megan Rae; my husband, Nick Ogle; and farmhand Brian Westgate; as well as the adorable Katy King, a young woman smarter about life than a tree full of owls. April Sutton's lend-a-hand attitude was indispensable in many ways, especially her work on recipes. Thanks, too, to Matt Ihm, Karin Smith, Rose Washam, Lisa Marie Martinez, Kathy Proctor, Brandi Roberts, and Carla Danielson for providing me with photo props.

Outside the circle of those who helped me create this book on paper are two salty, tough, irreverent Idaho men who helped me "live my one wild life," and I am eternally grateful to them. Unbeknownst to either of them, they were blazing a trail for me that would create who I am today.

Emil Keck

Emil Keck was already an institution in the U.S. Forest Service when I showed up for duty at the most remote ranger station in the Lower 48, arriving in 1976 via a two-seater Cessna that landed in Emil's horse pasture. Tool box in hand, I became the Selway-Bitterroot's first female wilderness station guard. Emil was already a living legend by the time I arrived, and even though he was always telling upper management where they could put it, he was eventually praised at its highest levels, his leadership skills unparalleled, his wilderness ethics unmatched. The bureaucrats who gave Emil Keck grief because of his outspoken ways will leave few marks, but Emil and his passion for wilderness will last forever. Although his style was harsh and painfully direct at times, the two years I spent working with him twenty-five miles from the end of a dirt road became the basis for my life's map—a code embedded with an intense can-do work ethic, tempered by an almost ministerial lend-a-hand attitude. When my biological clock ticked loud enough to disturb the silence, I left, telling him I aimed to have a son and name him Emil. Five years later, I had a son that I named Emil, born on Emil Keck's birthday. Emil Keck lived in the Selway country until his death, in 1990, at the age of seventy-seven.

MaryJane, Emil Keck, and Meg, 1981

Cecil D. Andrus, Idaho's four-term governor and former U.S. Secretary of the Interior, worked tirelessly to create designated wilderness areas throughout the West and Alaska during the era I lived and breathed wilderness. Through numerous additions to the national park system, the wilderness system, the wild rivers system, and national wildlife refuges, Andrus ensured the preservation of some 103 million acres in perpetuity. Those of us who are passionate about the need to preserve wilderness have benefited immeasurably from his Western style of politics when we've needed to take exception to public policy: take good aim and talk straight, Andrus style. Over the years, as I've lived in small remote towns throughout my state, his tough, strong stand on issues of preservation has touched the lives of every citizen I've known. Idahoans miss him. Heck, even Robert Redford says he misses having Andrus in office. On March 14, 2008, as this book was going to press, I was awarded the *Cecil D. Andrus Leadership Award for Sustainability and Conservation* in person by "Cece" himself. To say I'm honored isn't enough. Thank you, Cece, for the great green splotches that show up on my maps.

CECIL ANDRUS

Politics Western Style

CECIL D. ANDRUS
AND JOEL CONNELLY

MaryJane Butters, a woman of many hats, grew up in Utah in a family of seven that was ardently self-sufficient during the week—raising their own food and sewing all their own clothes—and nomadic on weekends, taking to the hills and sagebrush flats of the West for the purpose of bringing home wild food. Like nomadic natives, they set up camp, fished, hunted, slept on the ground, and fell into wild ways with natural grace.

Longing for fertile ground where she could raise her own flock of chickens, maybe a cow or two, and a family, she made her way north, working as a wilderness ranger, wrangler, fence builder, carpenter, forest fire lookout, and milkmaid.

Rooted now on her own five acres for the past twenty-two years (seven of those as a single mom), MaryJane, at age fifty-five, has accomplished everything she set out to achieve, including a few surprises. Fifteen years ago, she married her neighbor, Nick Ogle, a third-generation farmer. Together they raised four hard-working children, plus bees, chickens, goats, cows, peas, beans, hay, wheat, and every vegetable imaginable, including a biodiesel crop to fuel MaryJane's pink Mercedes Benz. She has cultivated future organic farmers in her apprenticeship program called Pay Dirt Farm School, bought an historic flour mill, and created the "Farmgirl Connection," a website that brings together thousands of women sharing their farmgirl dreams (www.maryjanesfarm.org), and MaryJane's Outpost Dispatch (www.maryjanesoutpost.org), where "out there" women post online. She is the editor of her own magazine, *MaryJanesFarm*, distributed nationwide, as well as a line of organic backpacking foods sold in camping stores throughout the United States and Canada.